E♭ Alto Clarinet

# HAL LEONARD Advanced BAND METHOD


BY HAROLD W. RUSCH

*with Special Studies by* Don McCathren


***For class . . . individual . . . full band instruction.***

PUBLISHED FOR

CONDUCTOR SCORE

C FLUTE

OBOE

B♭ CLARINET

E♭ ALTO CLARINET

B♭ BASS CLARINET

BASSOON

E♭ ALTO SAXOPHONE

B♭ TENOR SAXOPHONE

E♭ BARITONE SAXOPHONE

B♭ CORNET & TRUMPET

FRENCH HORN IN F

FRENCH HORN IN E♭ (MELLOPHONE)

TROMBONE

BARITONE T.C.

BARITONE B.C.

BASSES (TUBA)

DRUMS

# FINGERING CHART FOR E♭ ALTO CLARINET

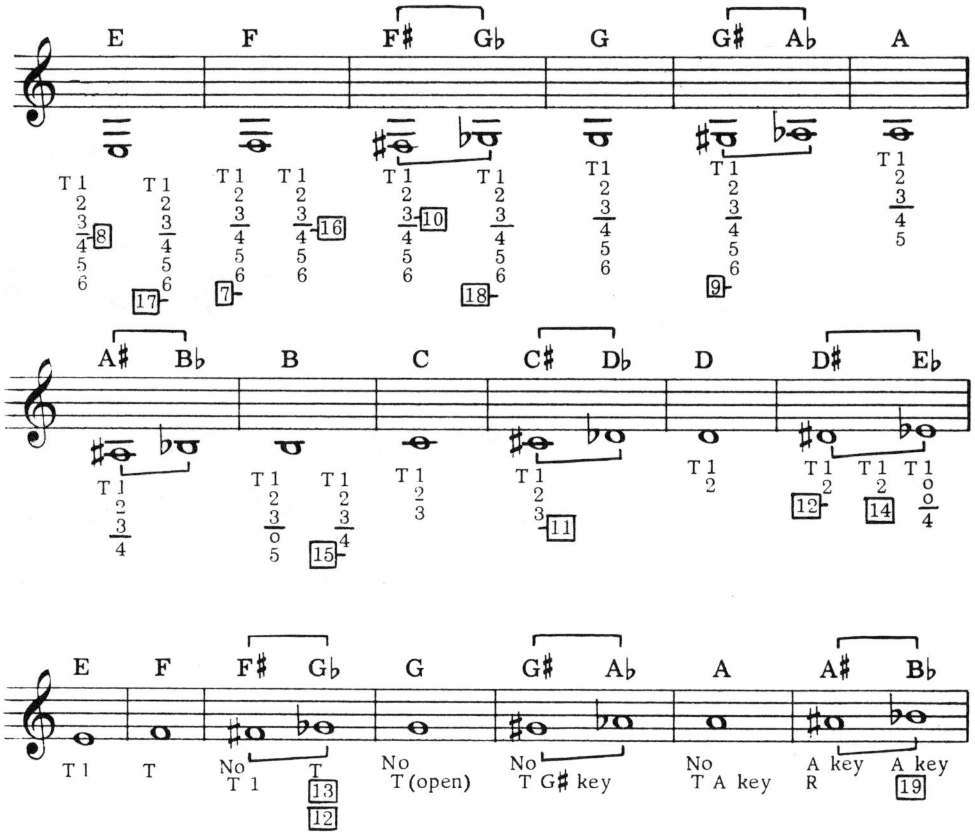


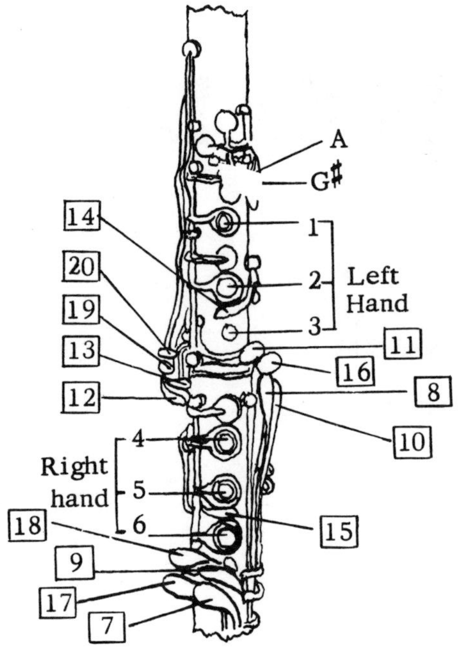


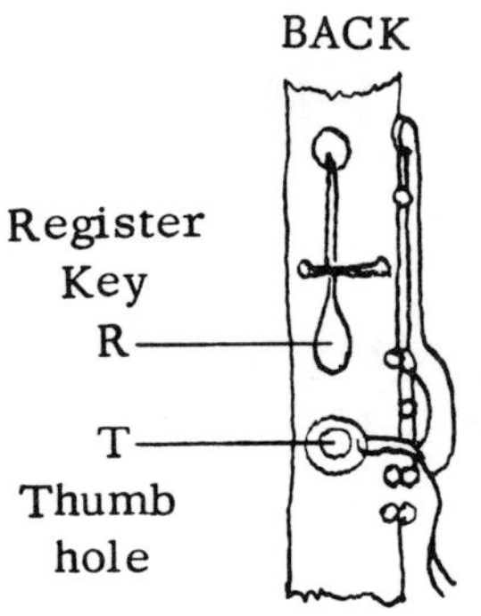


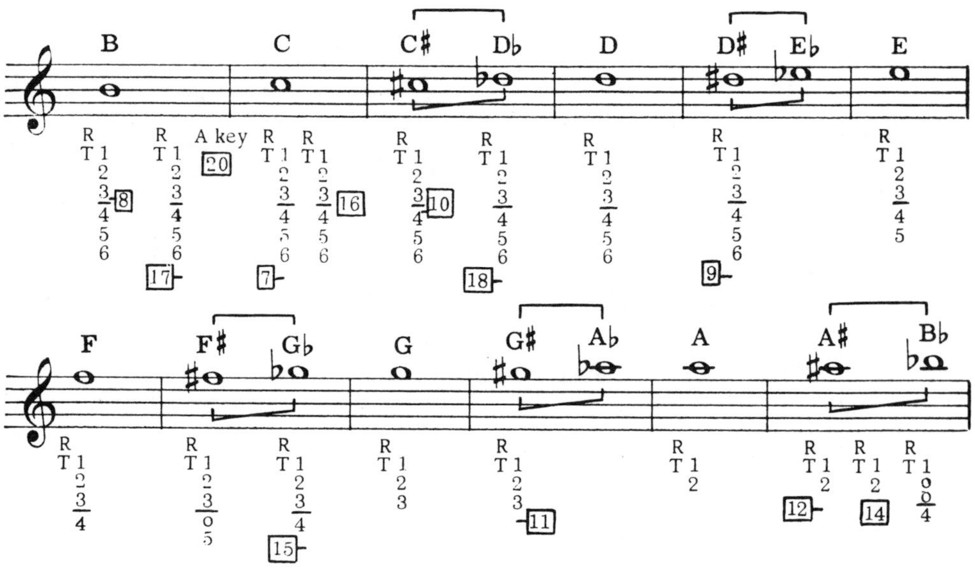


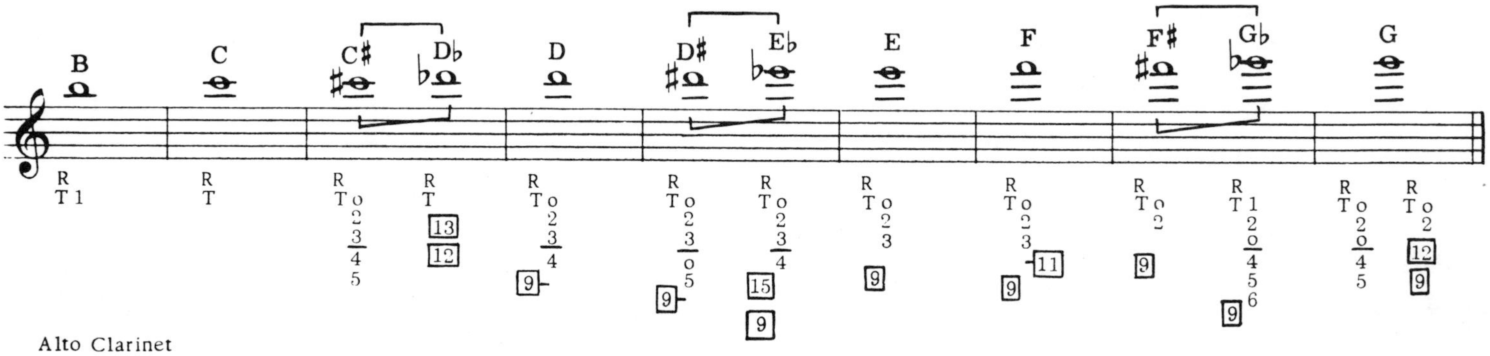

# G Major

(B♭ Concert)

Breathing and Warm Up

(1) 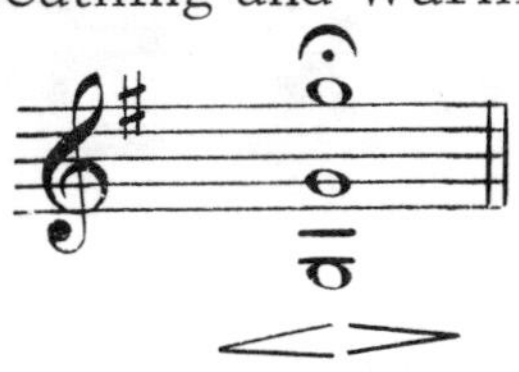

1. Hold the tone for 10 counts.
2. Expel any air remaining in lungs.
3. Do not breathe for 10 counts.
4. Inhale.
5. Repeat the sequence.
6. Apply to playing the scale.

## Scale

(2) 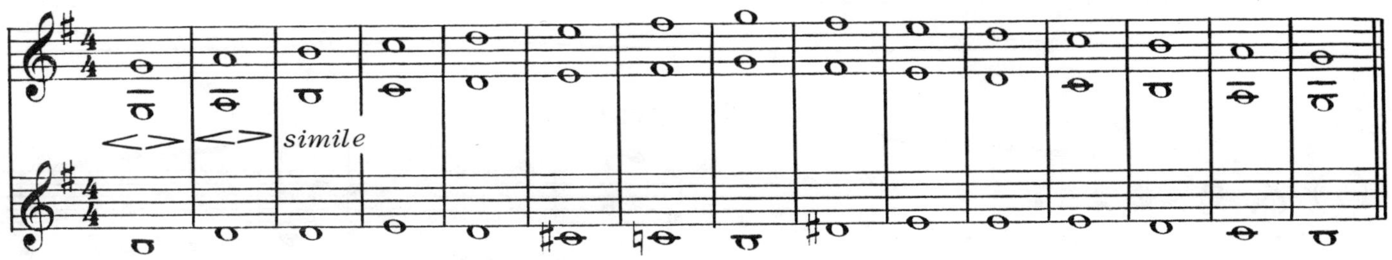


(3) 

## Scale Study

Rhythms 

Pares

(4) 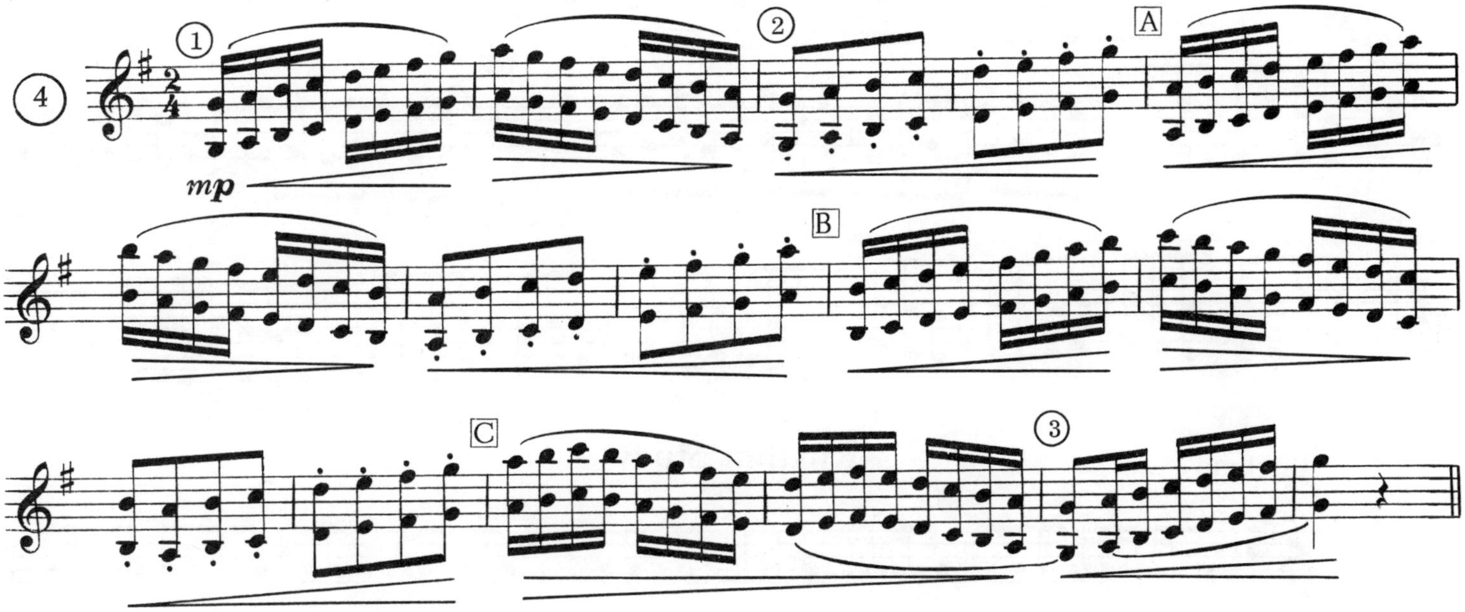

## Chord Study

## Chromatic

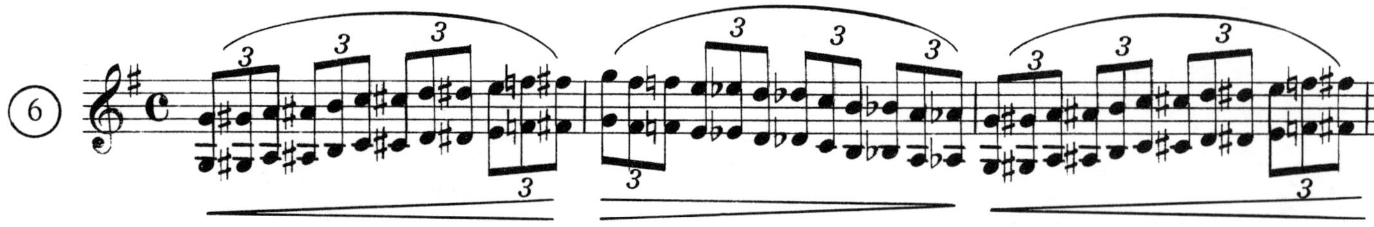


## Intervals

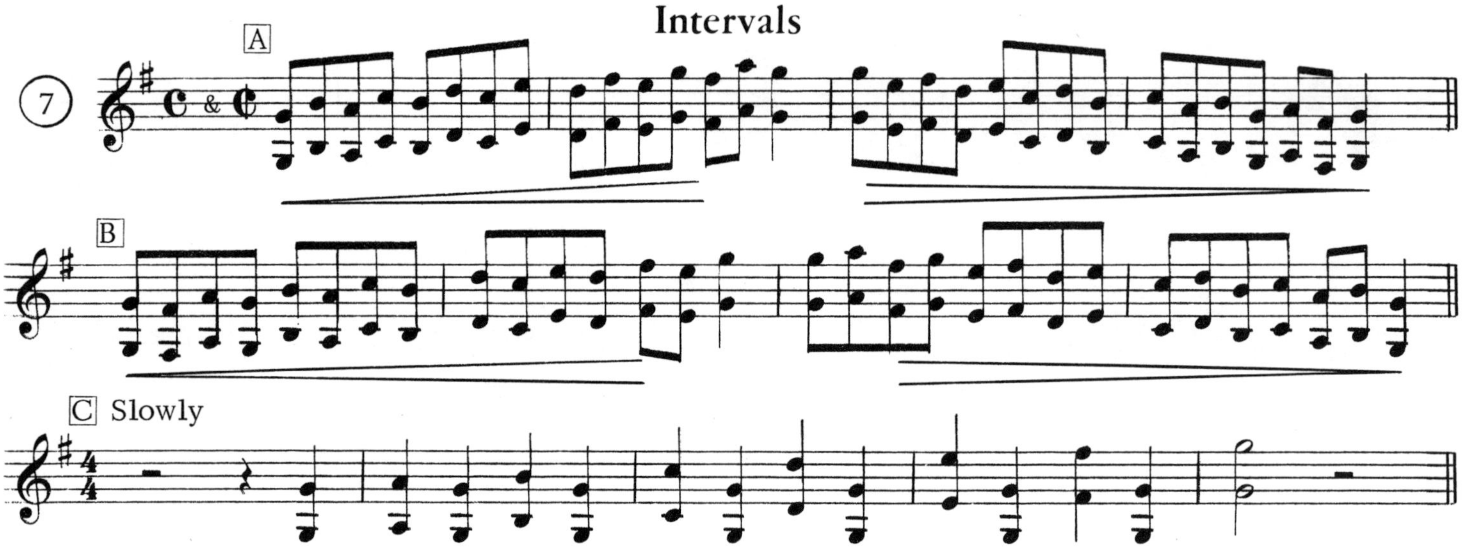


## Articulation Study

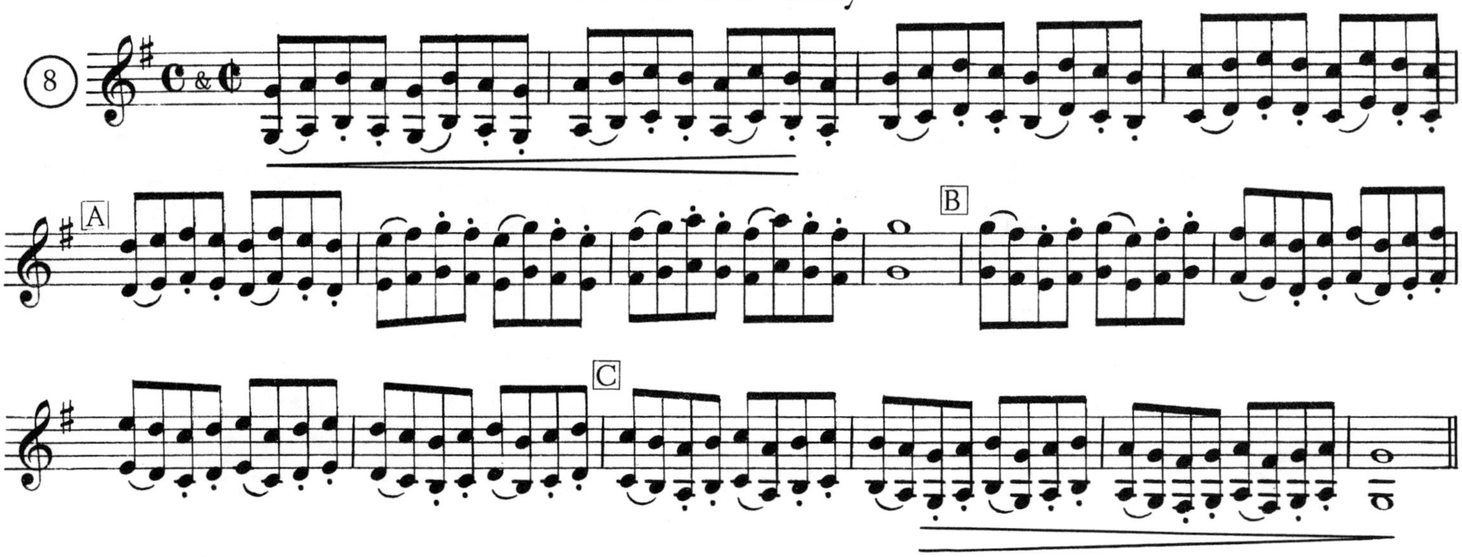


## Rhythm Study

Moderato
Arban
(adapted)
9
mp
sempre staccato
mf legato

## Etude

Embellishment-Refer to Ex. 148
Rhythms
Short grace note

Andante
Jancourt
(adapted)
10
p legato

## Accompaniment for Etude

## E Minor

(G Minor Concert)
(Relative to G Major)

Breathing and Warm Up

11

1. Hold the tone for 10 counts.
2. Expel any air remaining in lungs.
3. Do not breathe for 10 counts.
4. Inhale.
5. Repeat the sequence.
6. Apply to playing the scale.

## Scale

(Harmonic Minor)

12

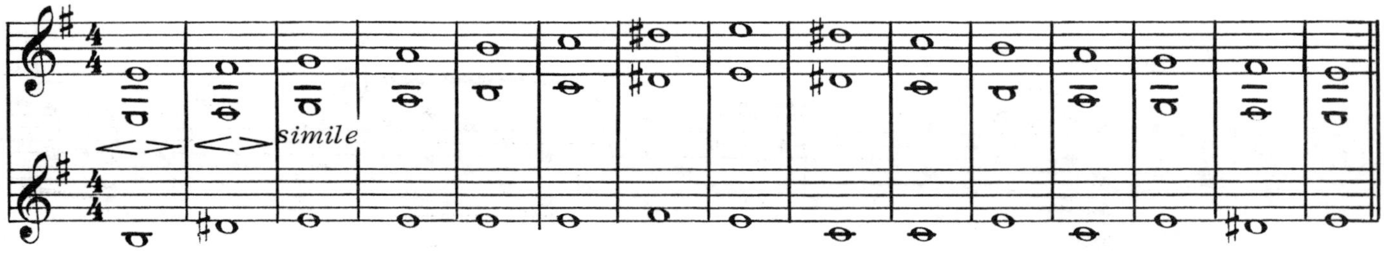


A Scale (Melodic Minor) B Tonic chord C Dominant chord

13

## Chord Study

14

* For Alto Clarinet with low E♭ Key.

## Intervals

15

## Etude

Rhythms

Allegretto

Barret
(adapted)

16

## Accompaniment for Etude

Allegretto

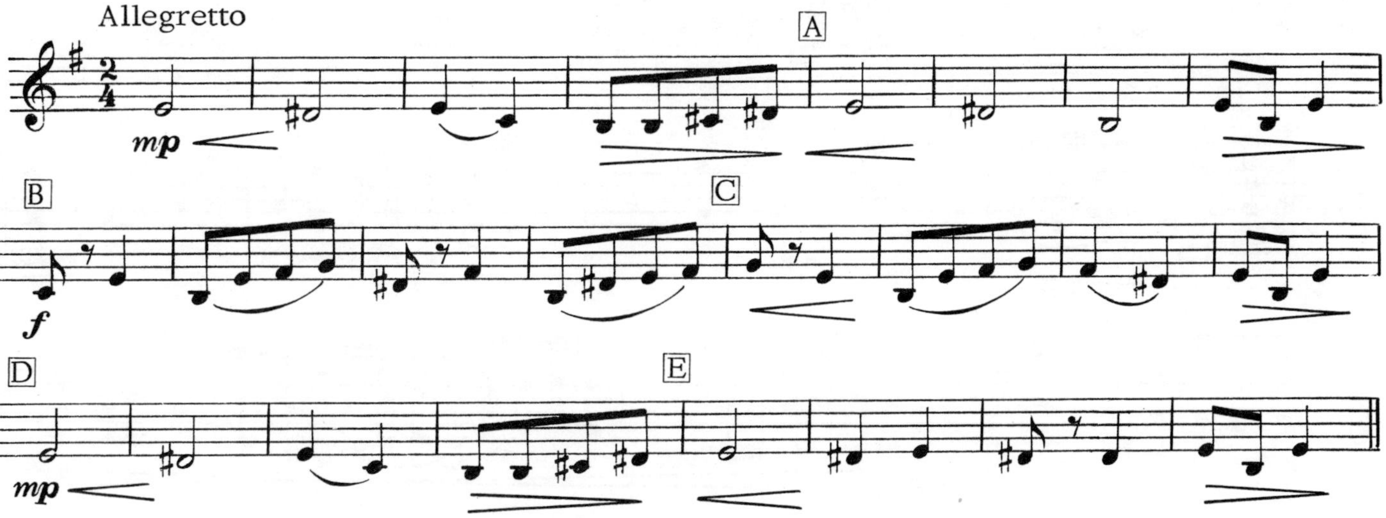

# C Major

(E♭ Concert)

Breathing and Warm Up

17 

1. Hold the tone for 10 counts.
2. Expel any air remaining in lungs.
3. Do not breathe for 10 counts.
4. Inhale.
5. Repeat the sequence.
6. Apply to playing the scale.

## Scale

18 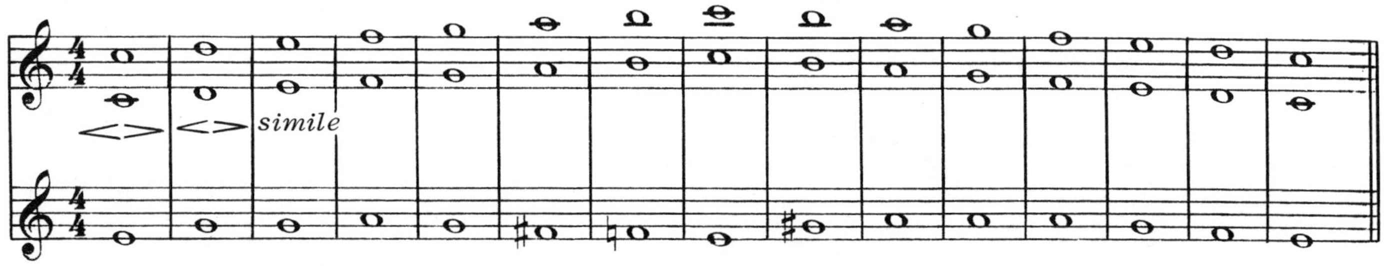


19 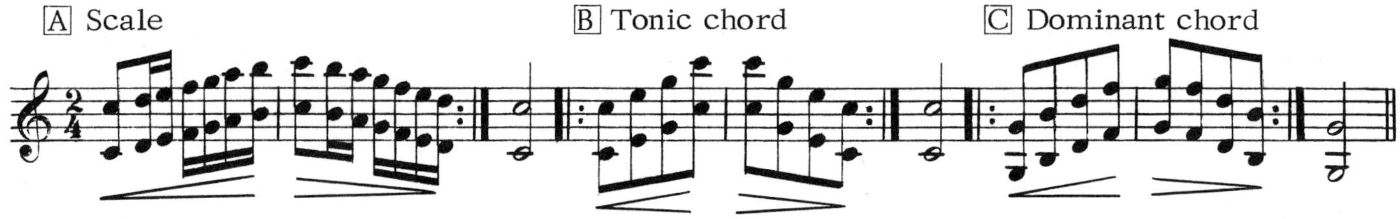


## Scale Study

Rhythms 

20 

## Chord Study

## Chromatic

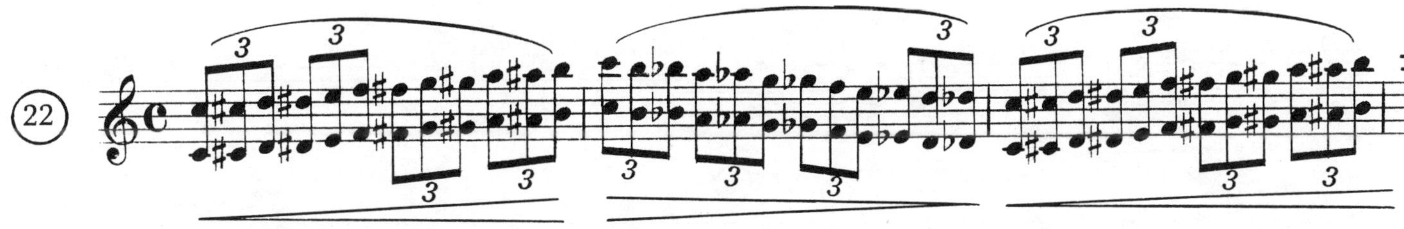


## Intervals

## Articulation Study

## Rhythm Study

## Etude

## Accompaniment for Etude

Moderato

## A Minor

(C Minor Concert)

(Relative to C Major)

Breathing and Warm Up

27 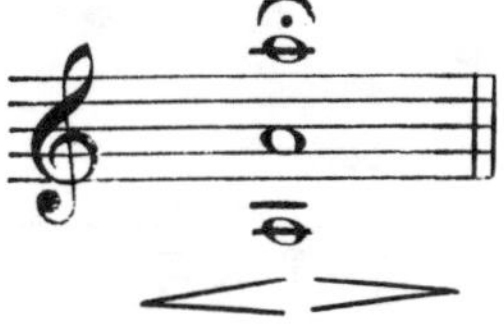

1. Hold the tone for 10 counts.
2. Expel any air remaining in lungs.
3. Do not breathe for 10 counts.
4. Inhale.
5. Repeat the sequence.
6. Apply to playing the scale.

## Scale

(Harmonic Minor)

28 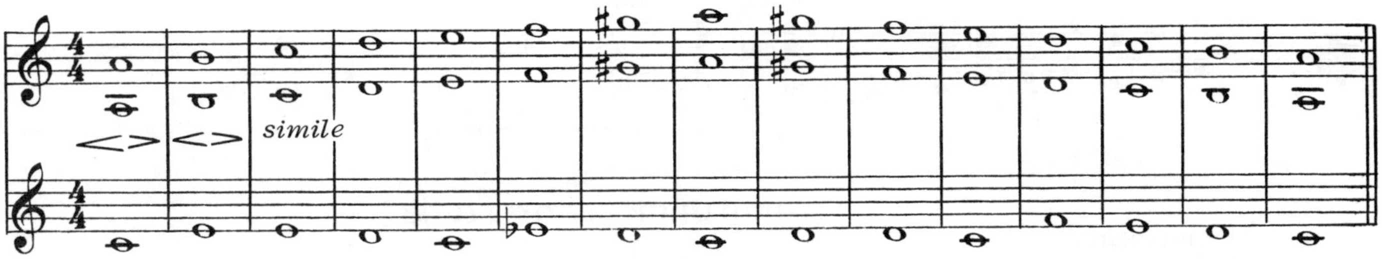


A Scale (Melodic Minor) B Tonic chord C Dominant chord

29 

## Chord Study

30 

## Intervals

## Etude

## Accompaniment for Etude

# F Major

(A♭ Concert)

Breathing and Warm Up

33
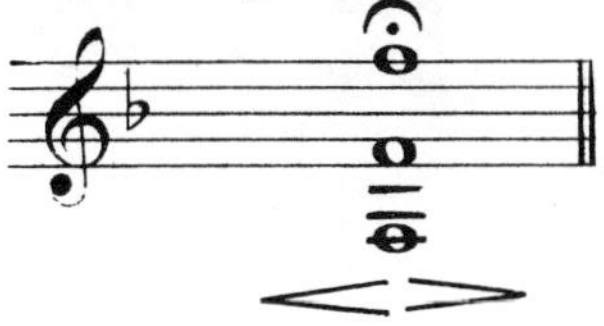

1. Hold the tone for 15 counts.
2. Expel any air remaining in lungs.
3. Do not breathe for 15 counts.
4. Inhale.
5. Repeat the sequence.
6. Apply to playing the scale.

## Scale

34
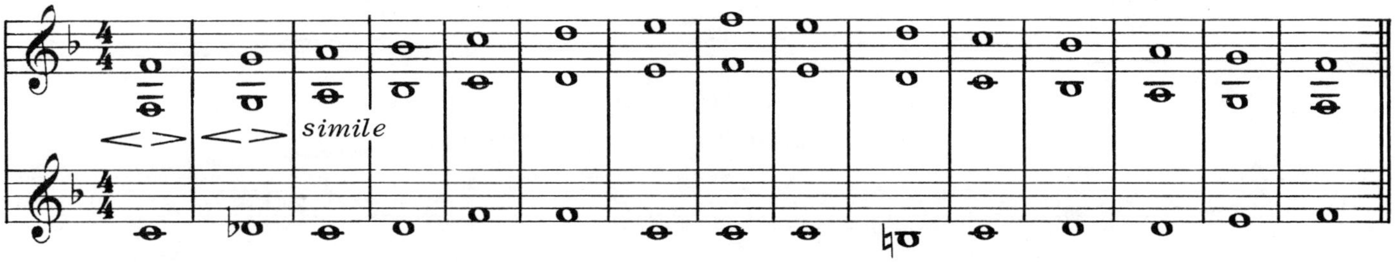


35
A Scale B Tonic chord C Dominant chord
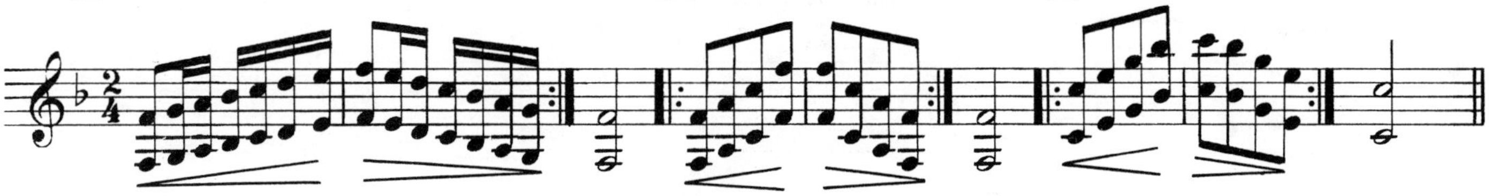

## Scale Study

Rhythms

36
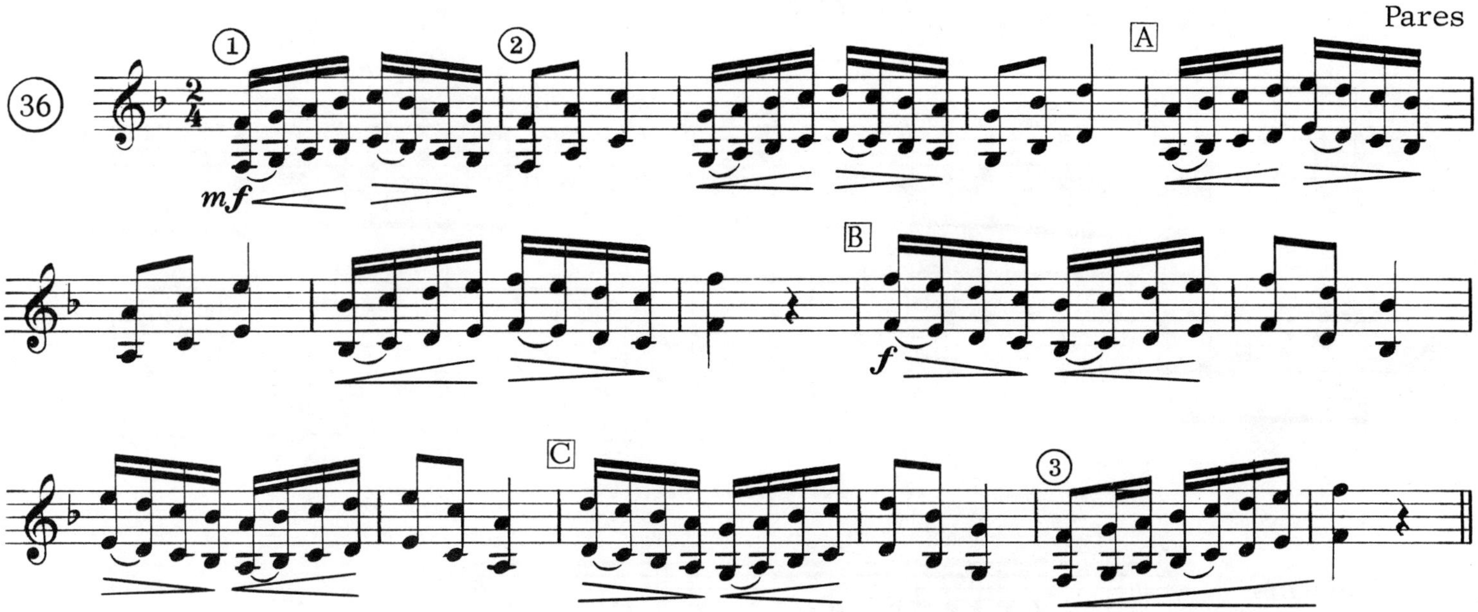

## Chord Study

(37)

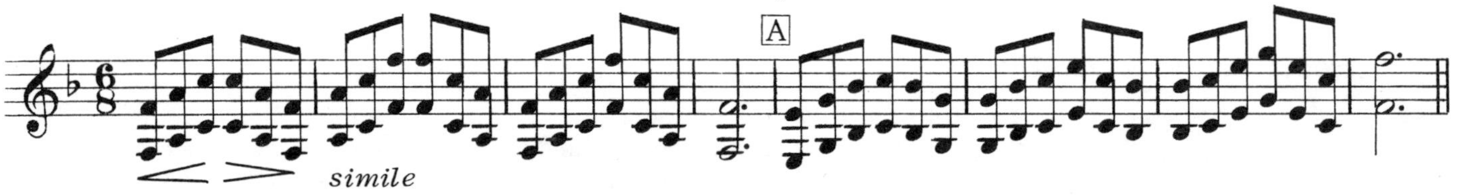


## Chromatic

(38)

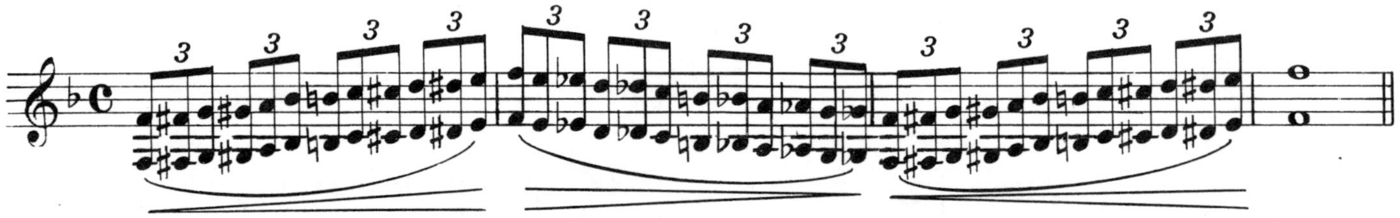


## Intervals

(39)

## Articulation Study

(40)

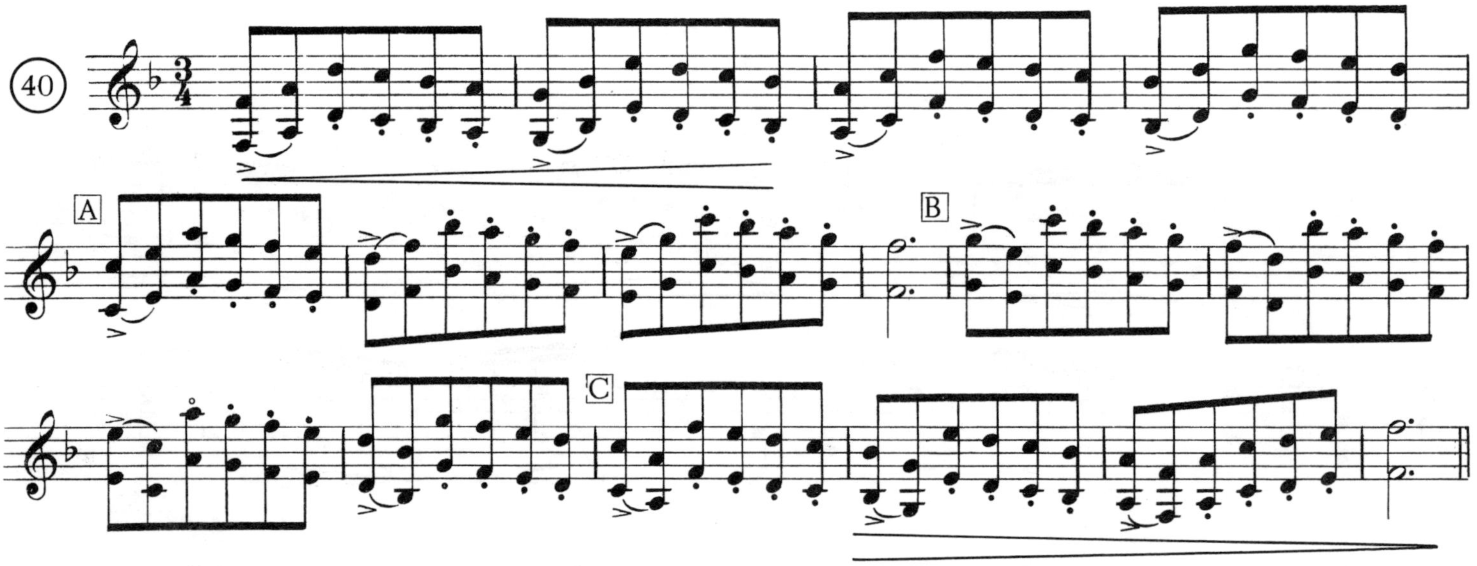


## Rhythm Study

Rhythms

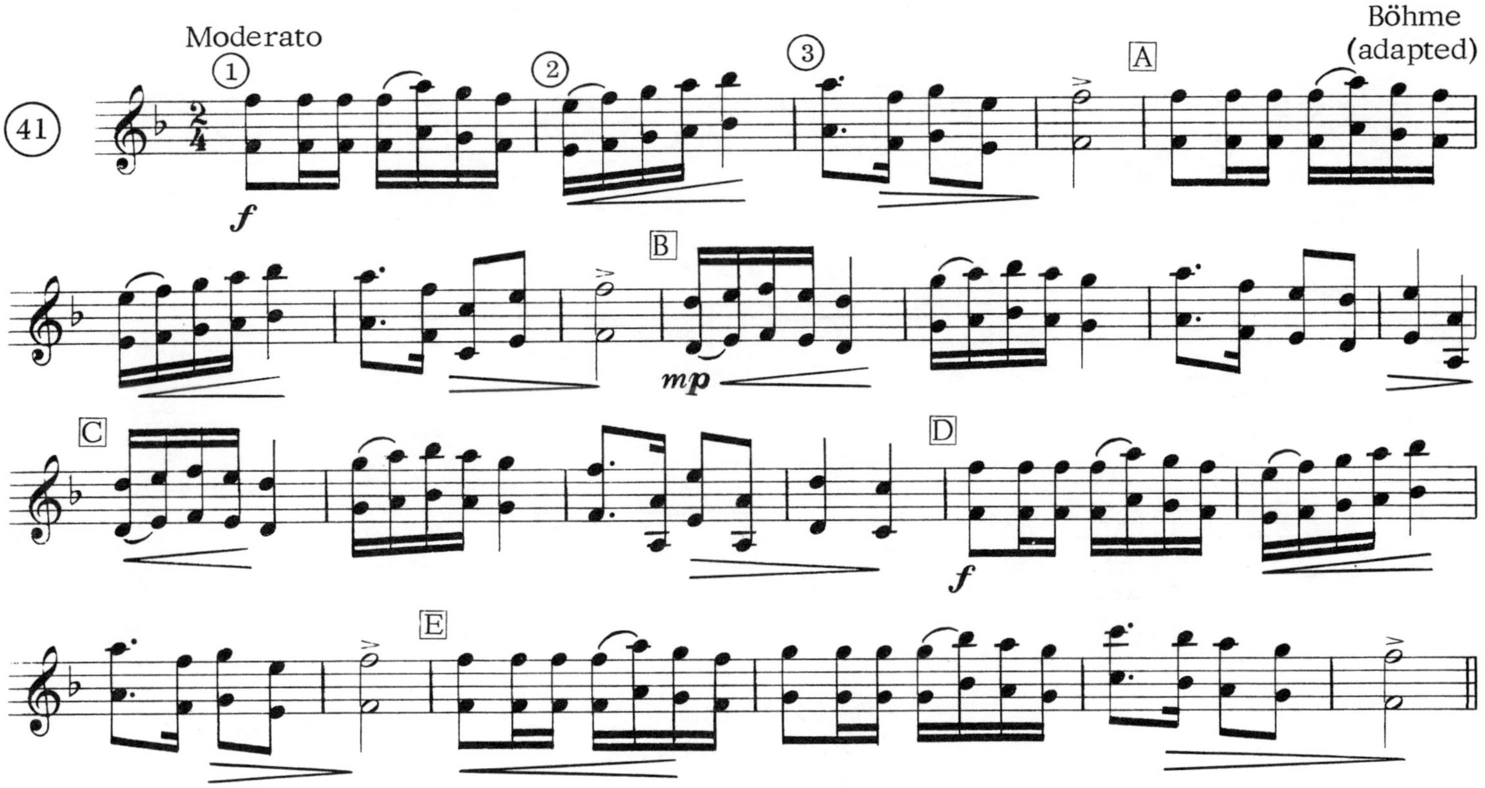
Moderato
Böhme
(adapted)
41
f
mp
A
B
C
D
E

## Etude

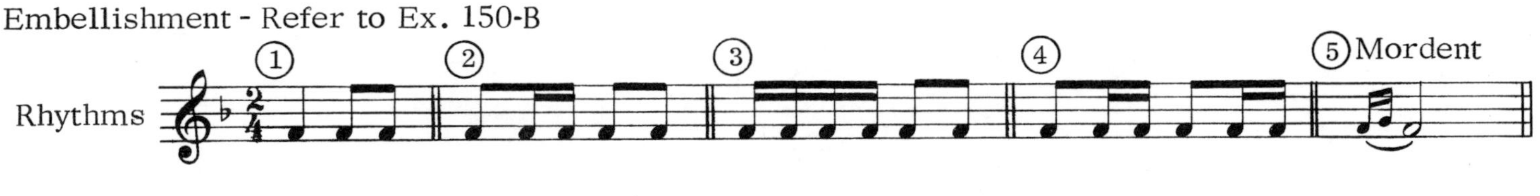
Embellishment - Refer to Ex. 150-B
Rhythms
5 Mordent

Allegretto
Barret
(adapted)
42
mf
f
cresc.
A
B
C
D
E

## Accompaniment for Etude

## D Minor

(F Minor Concert)
(Relative to F Major)

Breathing and Warm Up

43 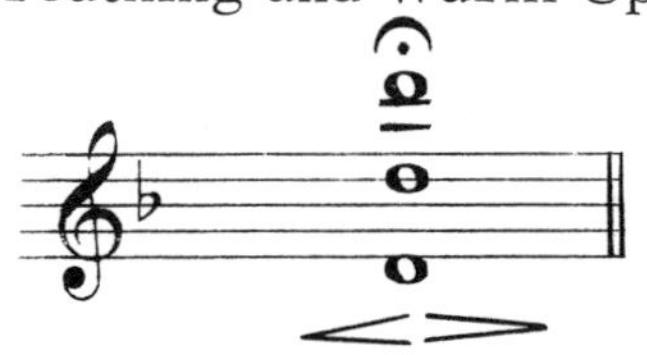

1. Hold the tone for 15 counts.
2. Expel any air remaining in lungs.
3. Do not breathe for 15 counts.
4. Inhale.
5. Repeat the sequence.
6. Apply to playing the scale.

### Scale

(Harmonic Minor)

44 

45 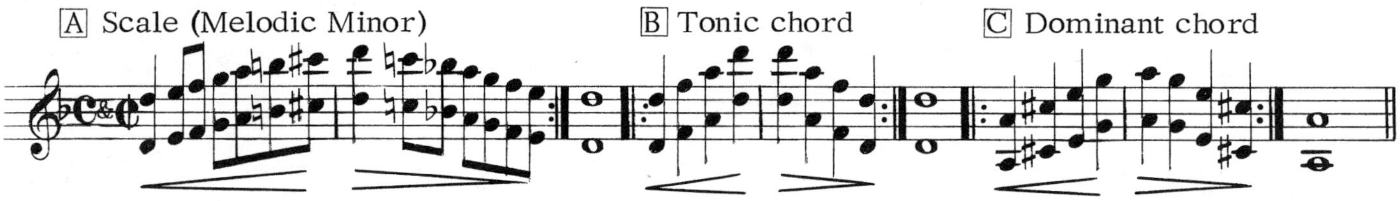


### Chord Study

46 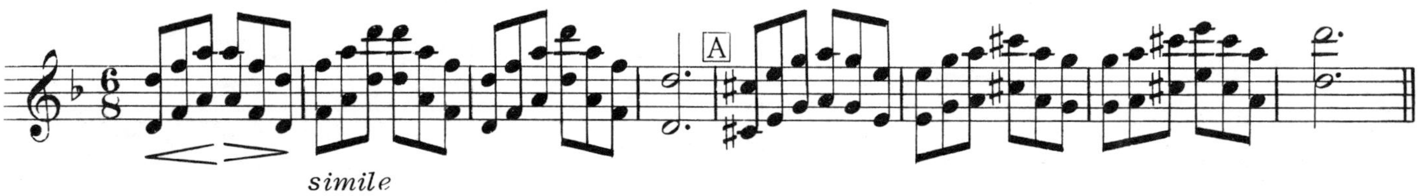

## Intervals

(47)

## Etude

Rhythms

Andantino

Lazarus
(adapted)

(48)

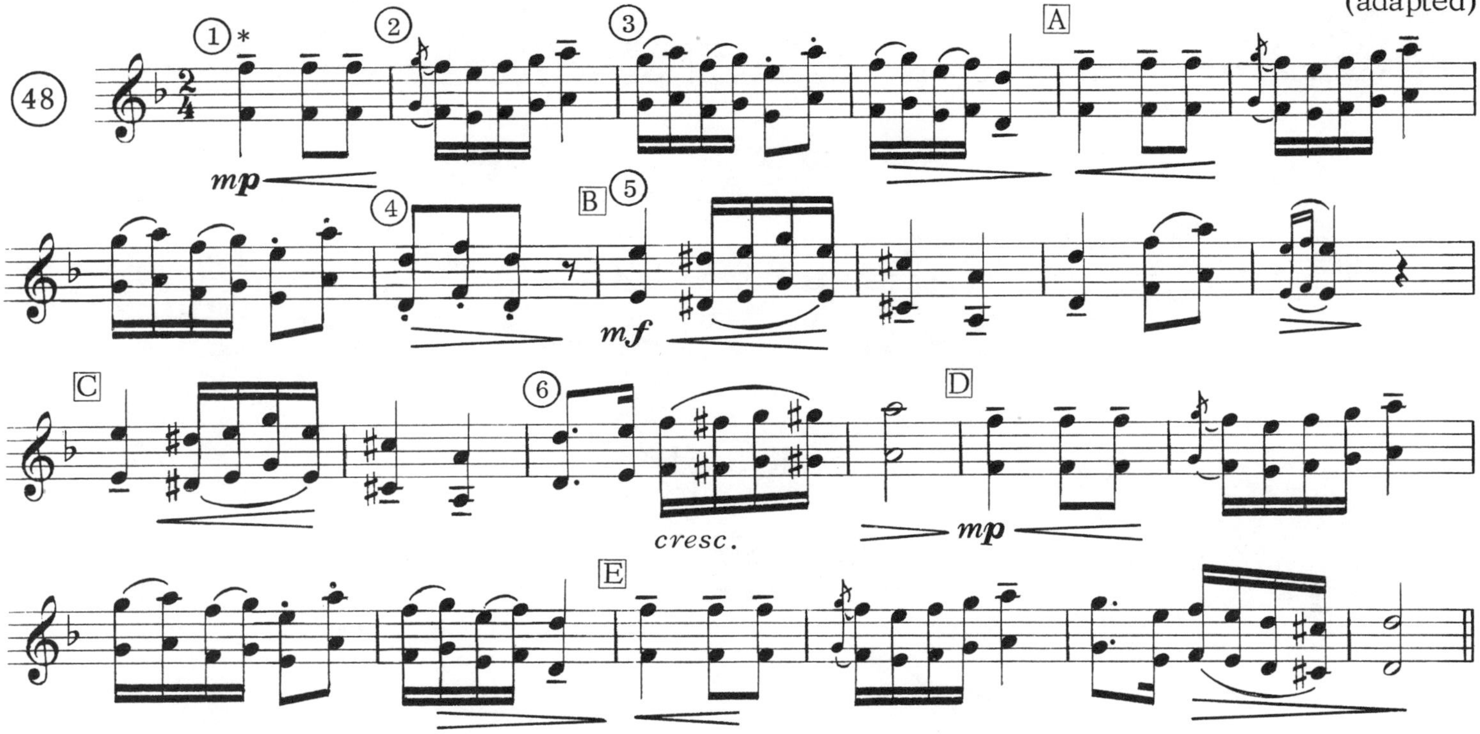


* Tenuto- Sustain tone for full value.

## Accompaniment for Etude

Andantino

# D Major
(F Concert)

Breathing and Warm Up

49 

1. Hold the tone for 15 counts.
2. Expel any air remaining in lungs.
3. Do not breathe for 15 counts.
4. Inhale.
5. Repeat the sequence.
6. Apply to playing the scale.

## Scale

50 

51 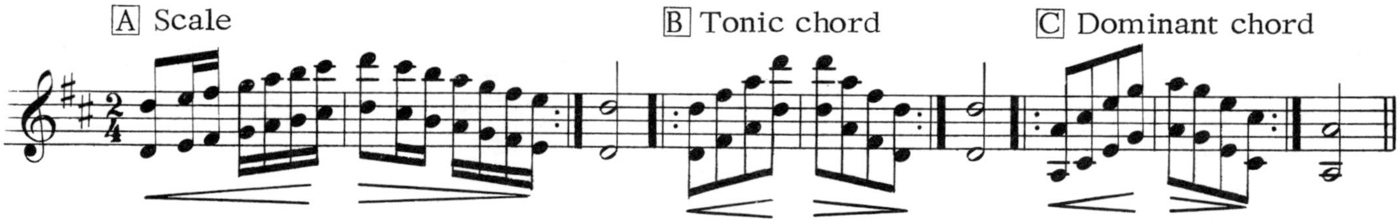


## Scale Study

Rhythms 

Pares (adapted)

52 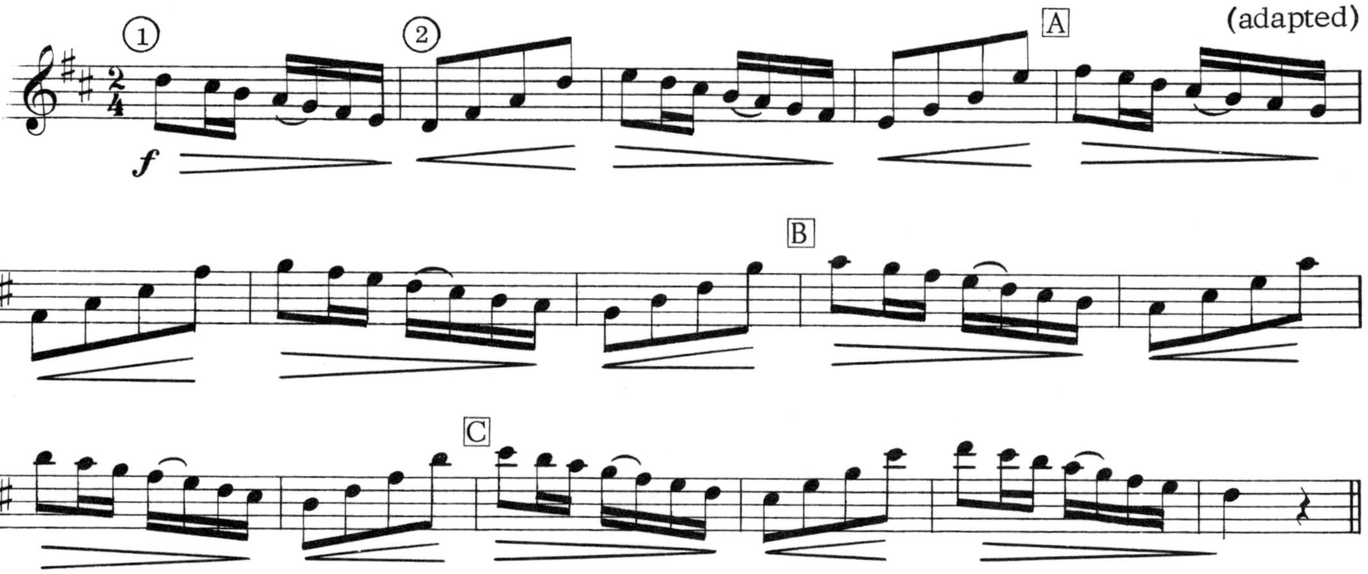

## Chord Study

53

## Chromatic

54
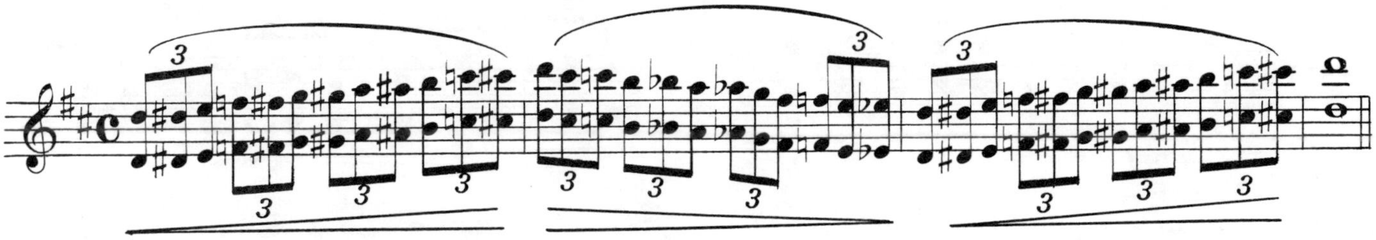

## Intervals

55

## Articulation Study

56

## Rhythm Study

Rhythms

Moderato

Jancourt
(adapted)

## Etude

Rhythms

Allegretto

Gatti
(adapted)

## Accompaniment for Etude

## B Minor

(D Minor Concert)
(Relative to D Major)

Breathing and Warm Up

59 

1. Hold the tone for 15 counts.
2. Expel any air remaining in lungs.
3. Do not breathe for 15 counts.
4. Inhale.
5. Repeat the sequence.
6. Apply to playing the scale.

## Scale

(Harmonic Minor)

60 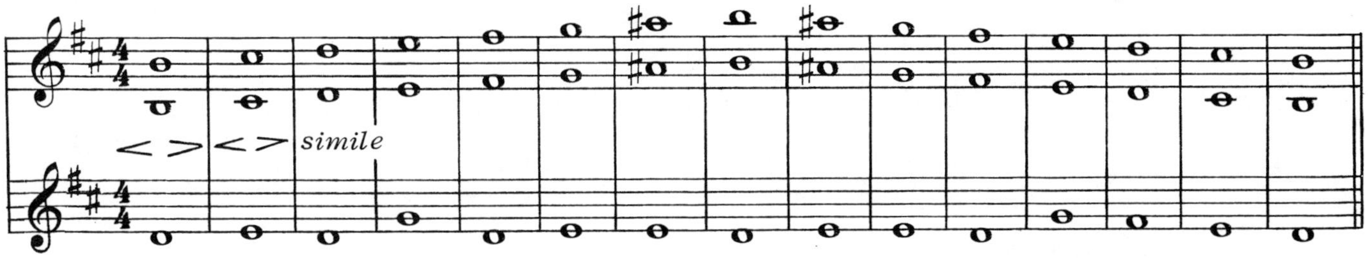


A Scale (Melodic Minor) — B Tonic chord — C Dominant chord

61 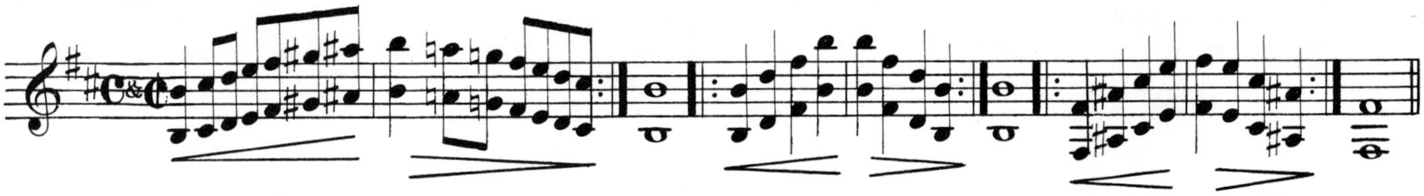

## Chord Study

62 

## Intervals

63

## Etude

Rhythms

Soussmann
(adapted)

64
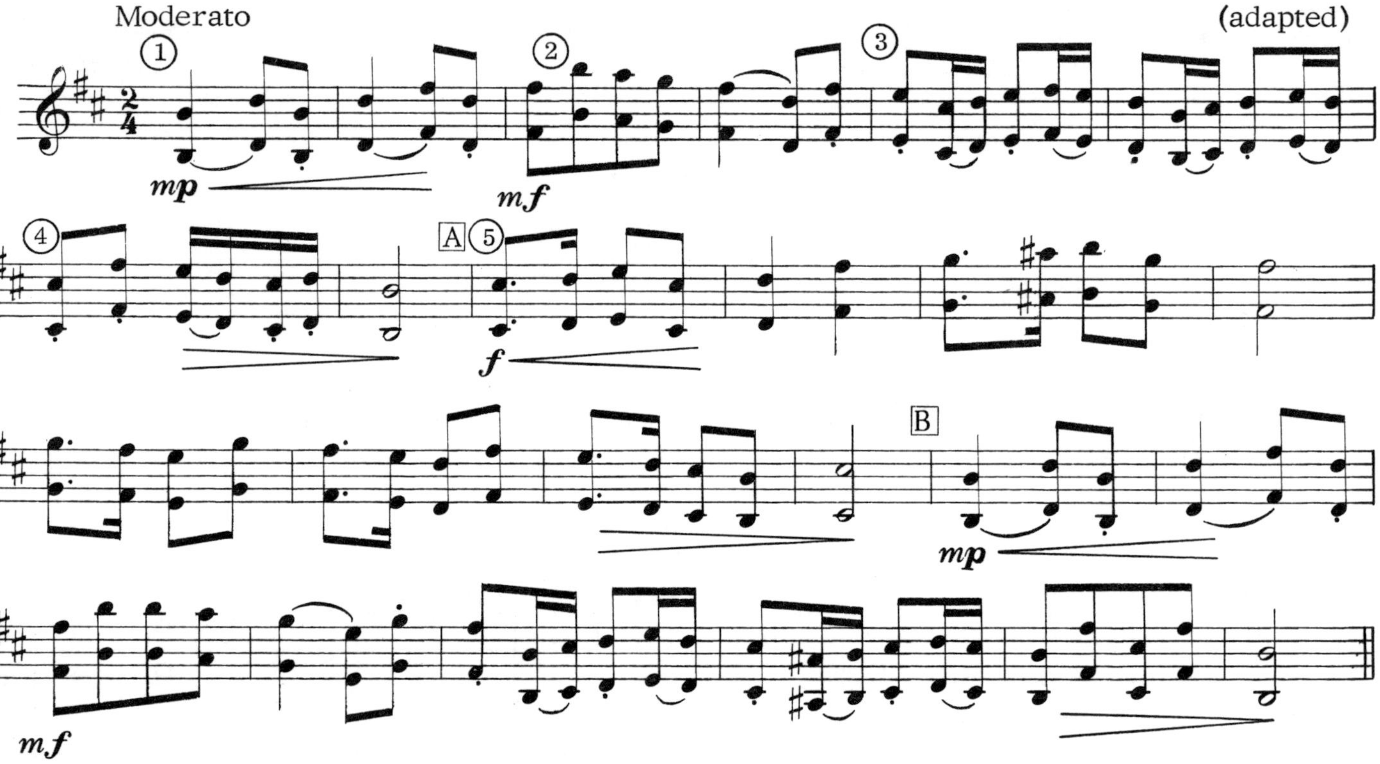


## Accompaniment for Etude

# A Major

(C Concert)

## Breathing and Warm Up

65 

1. Hold the tone for 15 counts.
2. Expel any air remaining in lungs.
3. Do not breathe for 15 counts.
4. Inhale.
5. Repeat the sequence.
6. Apply to playing the scale.

## Scale

66 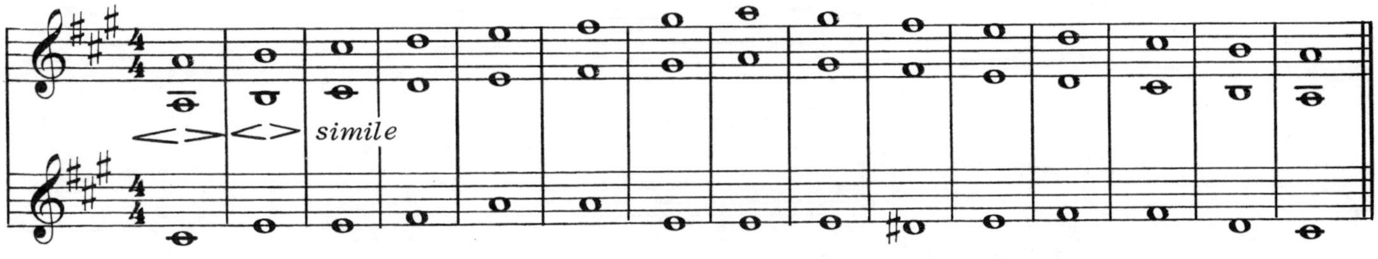


67 A Scale B Tonic chord C Dominant chord

## Scale Study

Rhythms 

Pares (adapted)

68 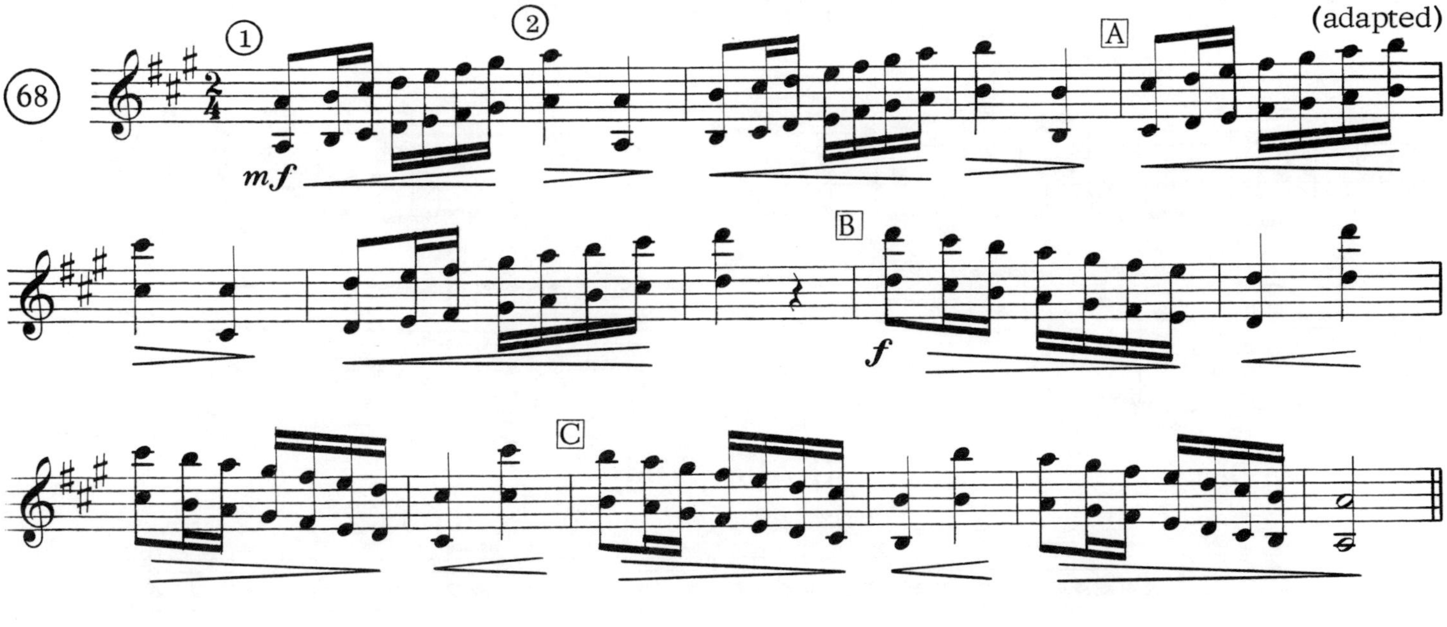

## Chord Study

## Chromatic

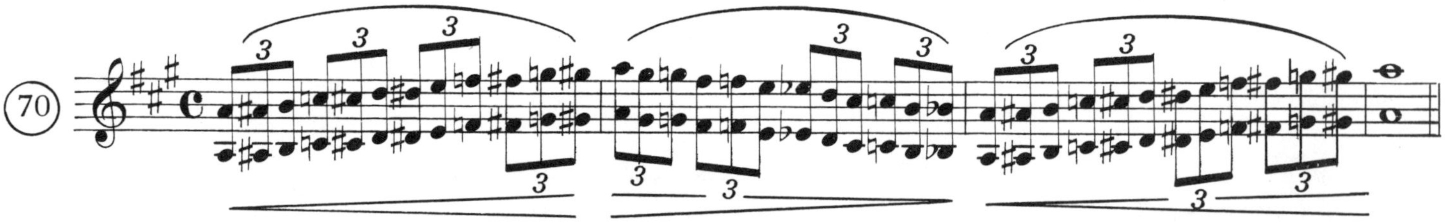


## Intervals

## Articulation Study

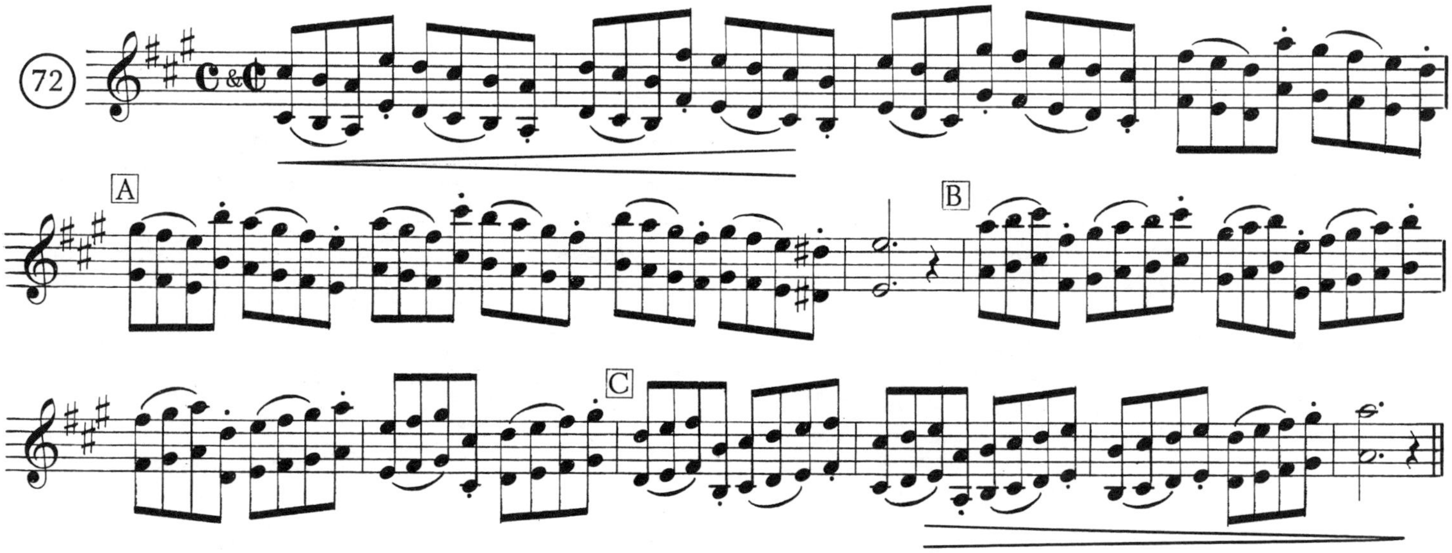


Rhythms

## Rhythm Study

Moderato

Pietzsch (adapted)

73

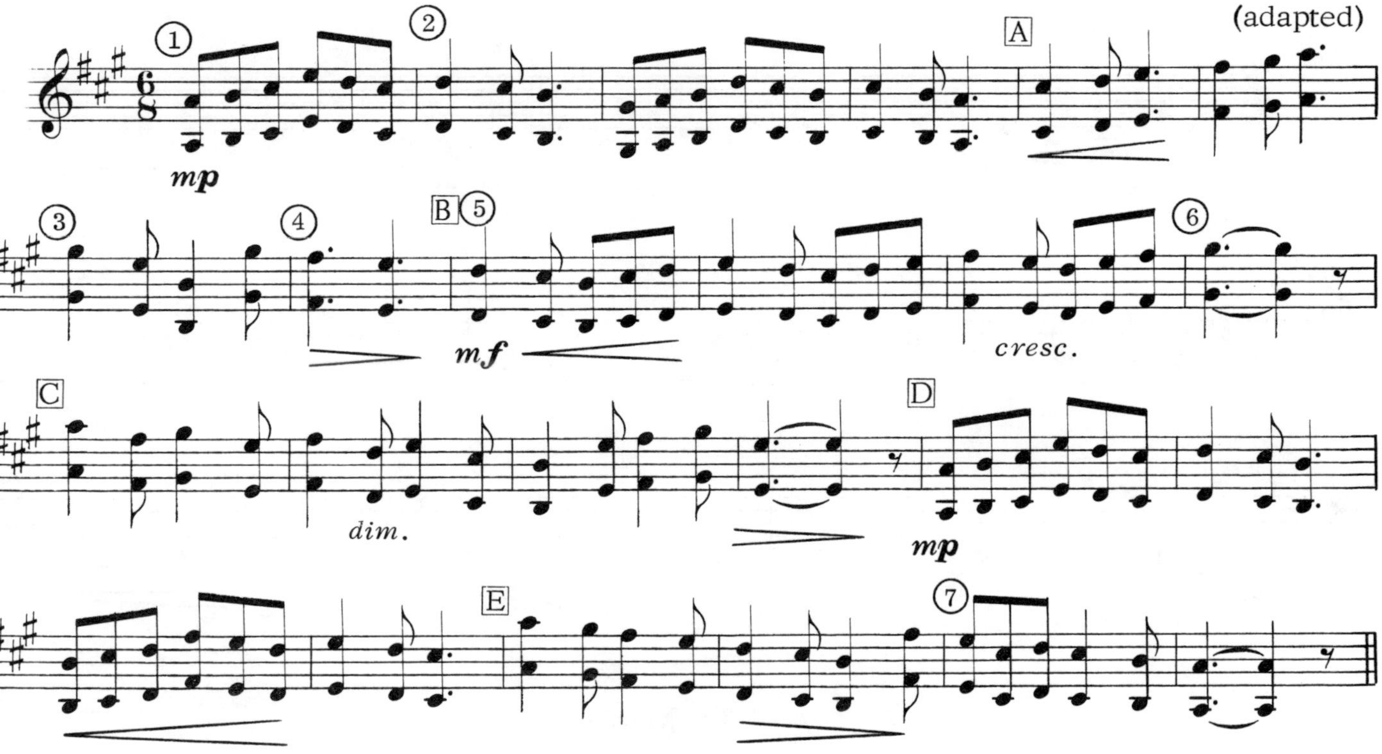

## Etude

Rhythms

Mordent

Allegretto

Fedorow (adapted)

74

## Accompaniment for Etude

Allegretto

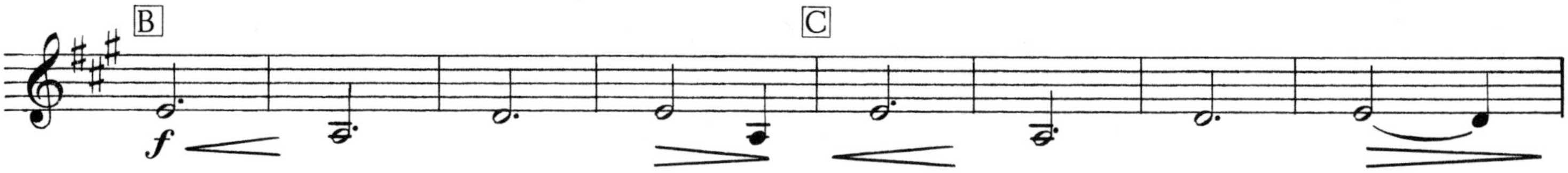

## F♯ Minor

(A Minor Concert)
(Relative to A Major)

Breathing and Warm Up

75

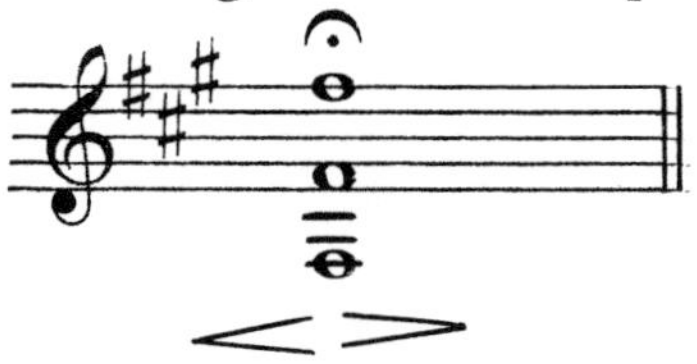

1. Hold the tone for 15 counts.
2. Expel any air remaining in lungs.
3. Do not breathe for 15 counts.
4. Inhale.
5. Repeat the sequence.
6. Apply to playing the scale.

## Scale

(Harmonic Minor)

76

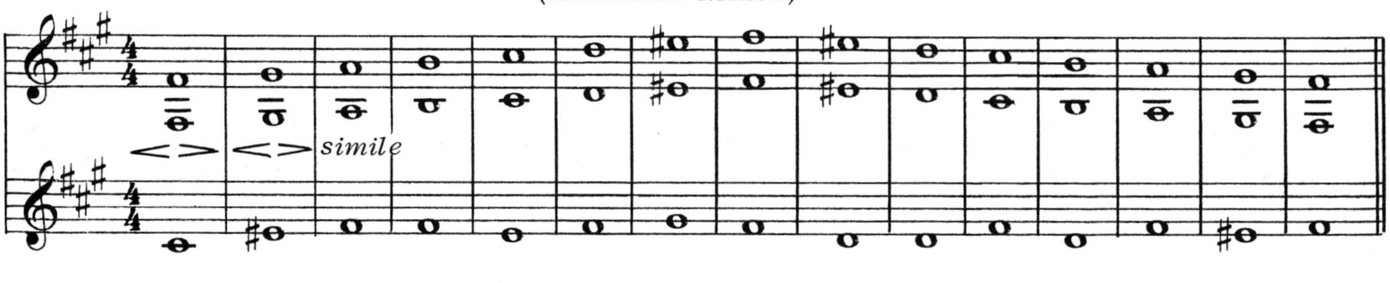


A Scale (Melodic Minor) B Tonic chord C Dominant chord

77

## Chord Study

78

## Intervals

79 

## Etude

Rhythms 

Barret
(adapted)

Allegretto

80 

## Accompaniment for Etude

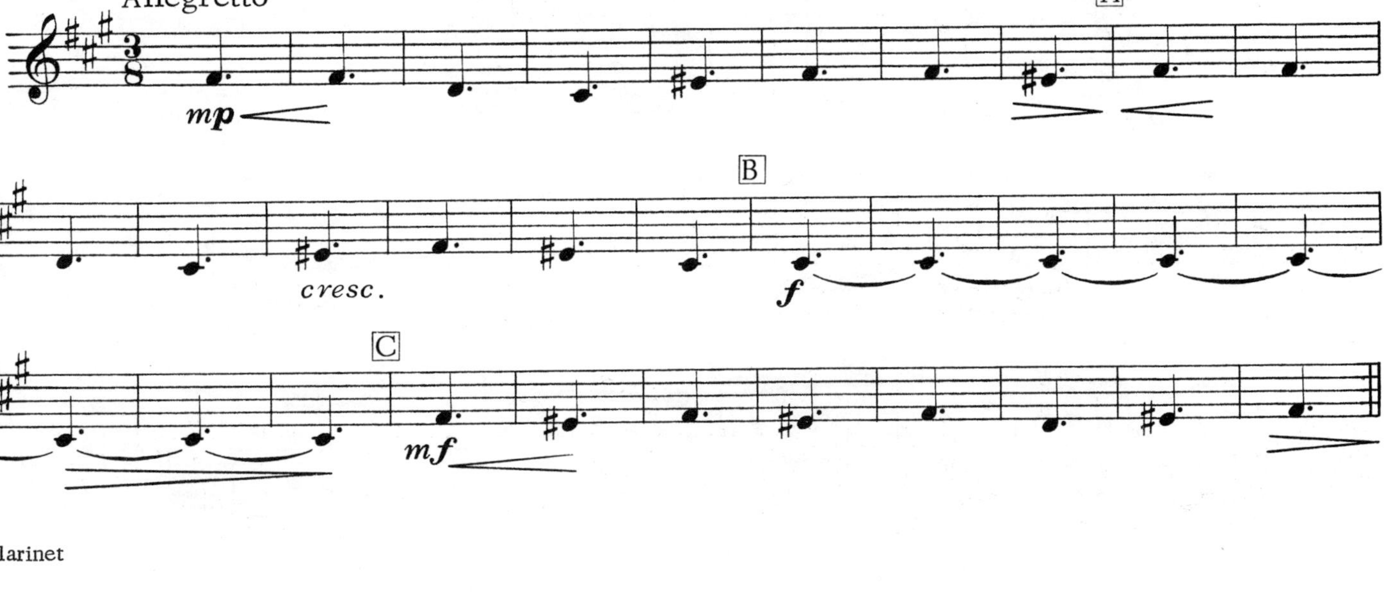

# B♭ Major

(D♭ Concert)

Breathing and Warm Up

81 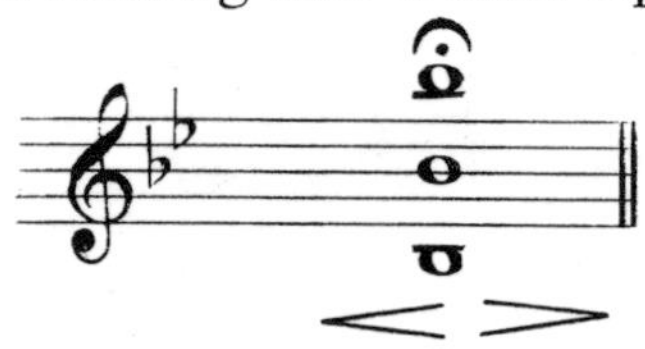

1. Hold the tone for 20 counts.
2. Expel any air remaining in lungs.
3. Do not breathe for 20 counts.
4. Inhale.
5. Repeat the sequence.
6. Apply to playing the scale.

## Scale

82 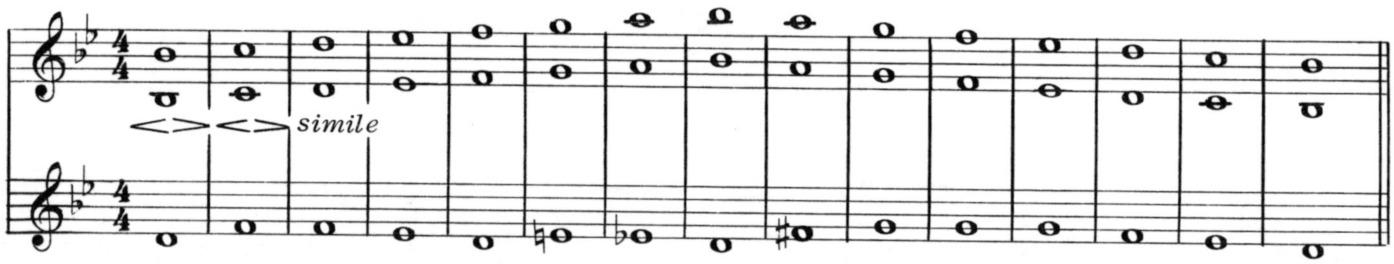


A Scale — B Tonic chord — C Dominant chord

83 

## Scale Study

Rhythms 

84 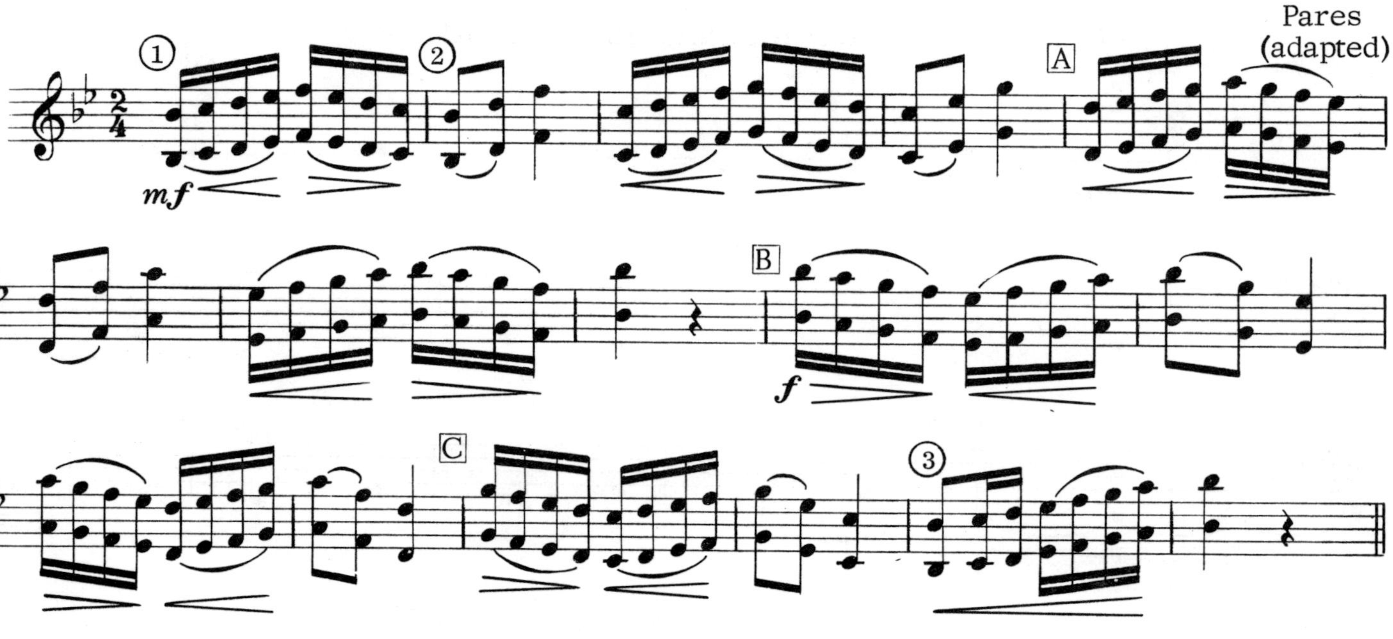

## Chord Study

## Chromatic

## Intervals

## Articulation Study

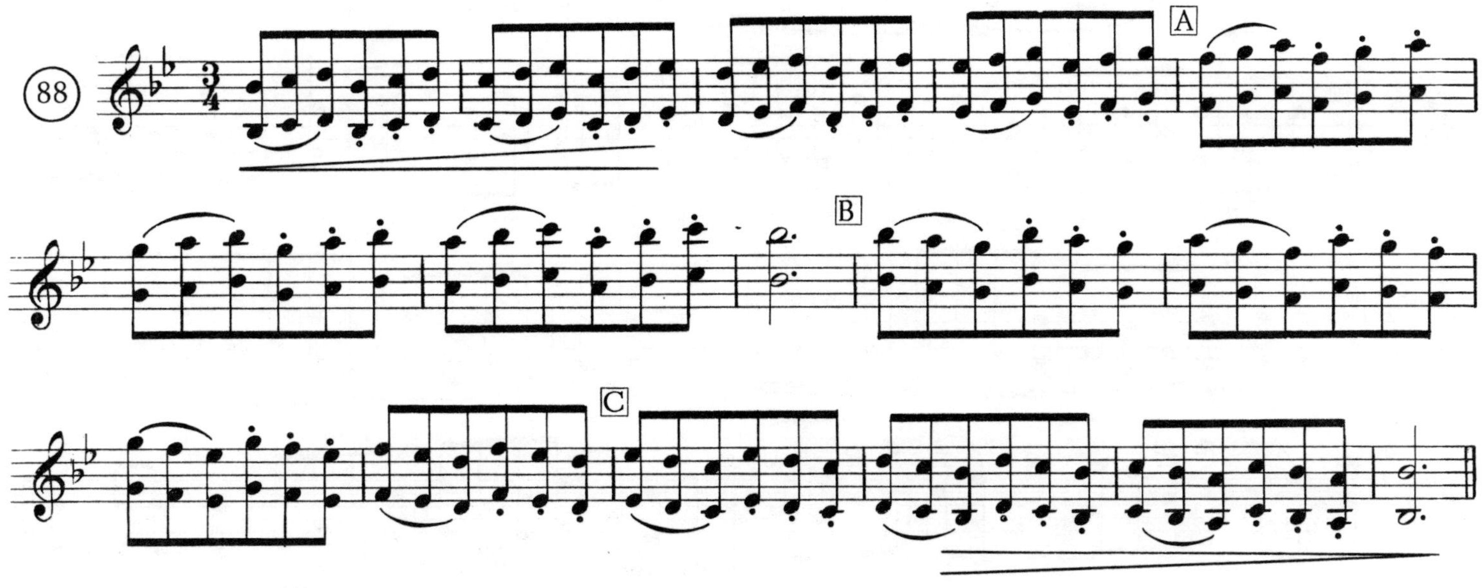

# Rhythm Study

Rhythms

Moderato

Jancourt
(adapted)

89

# Etude

Rhythms

Allegretto

Böhme
(adapted)

90

## Accompaniment for Etude

## G Minor

(B♭ Minor Concert)

(Relative to B♭ Major)

Breathing and Warm Up

91

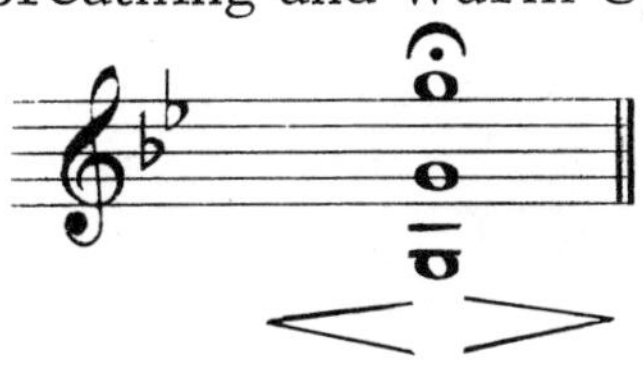

1. Hold the tone for 20 counts.
2. Expel any air remaining in lungs.
3. Do not breathe for 20 counts.
4. Inhale.
5. Repeat the sequence.
6. Apply to playing the scale.

## Scale

(Harmonic Minor)

92

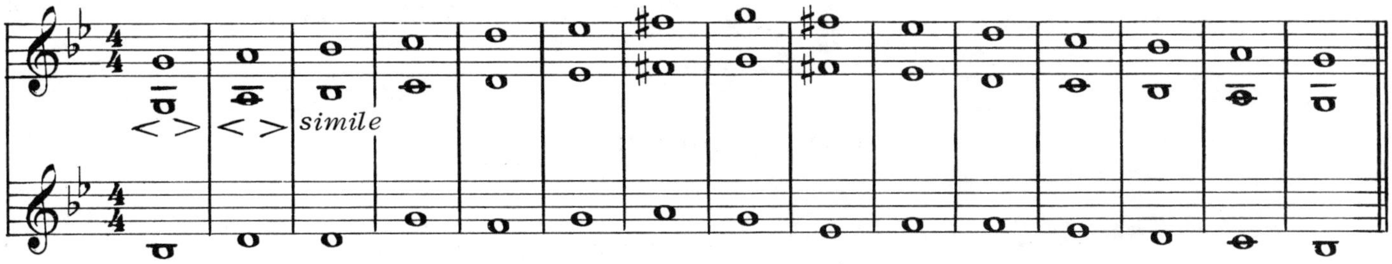


A Scale (Melodic Minor) B Tonic chord C Dominant chord

93

## Chord Study

94

## Intervals

95

## Etude

Rhythms

Moderato

Makin (adapted)

96

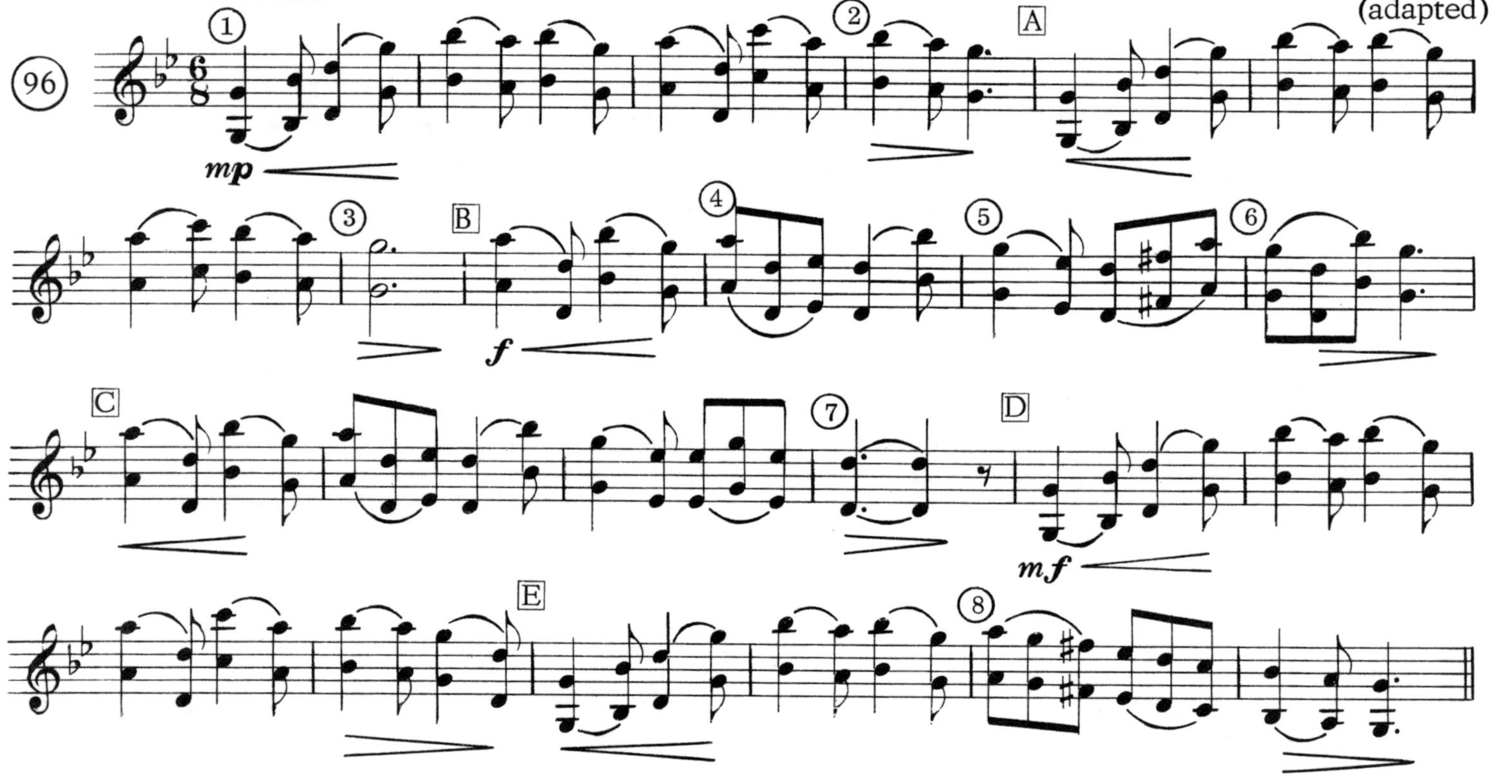

## Accompaniment for Etude

Moderato

# E Major

(G Concert)

Breathing and Warm Up

(97)

1. Hold the tone for 20 counts.
2. Expel any air remaining in lungs.
3. Do not breathe for 20 counts.
4. Inhale.
5. Repeat the sequence.
6. Apply to playing the scale.

## Scale

(98)

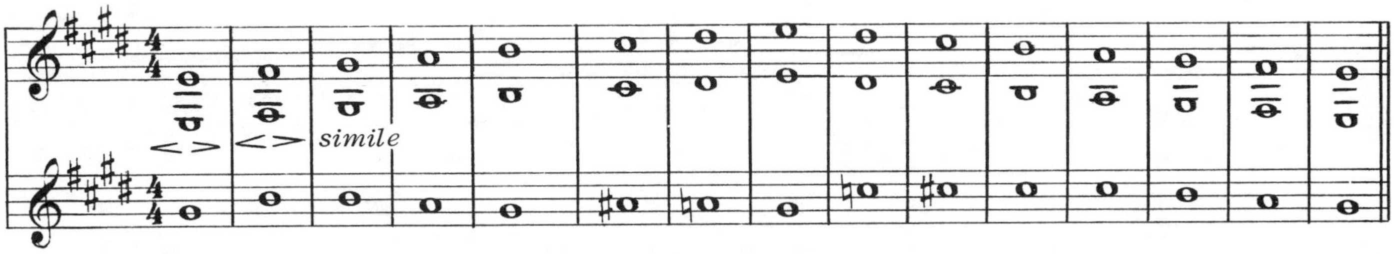


(99)

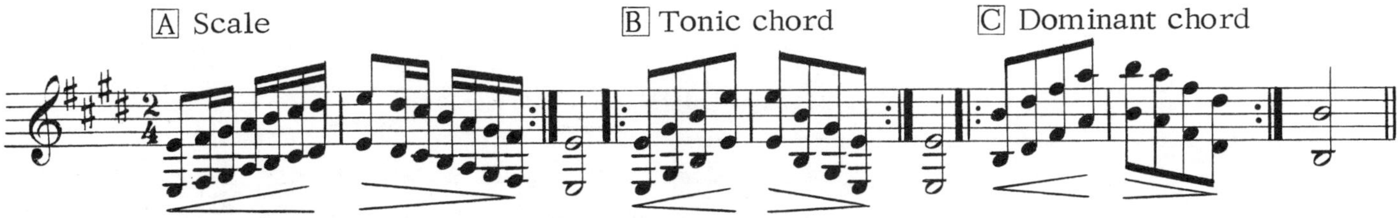


## Scale Study

Rhythms

Pares (adapted)

(100)

## Chord Study

(101)

* For Alto Clarinet with low E♭ Key.

## Chromatic

(102)

## Intervals

(103)

* For Alto Clarinet with low E♭ Key.

## Articulation Study

(104)

## Rhythm Study

Rhythms

Andantino

Alphonse (adapted)

(105)

## Etude

Rhythms

Soussmann
(adapted)

106

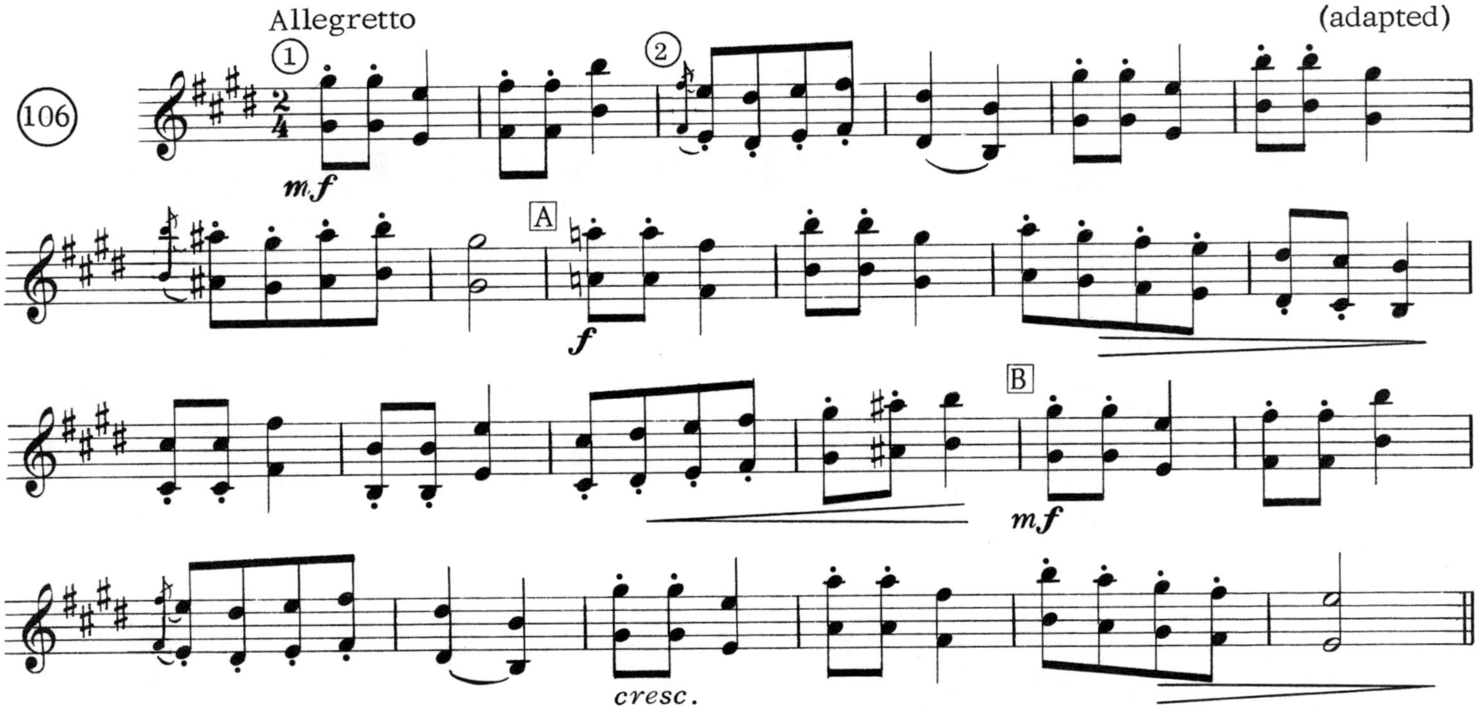


## Accompaniment for Etude

# C♯ Minor

(E Minor Concert)
(Relative to E Major)

## Breathing and Warm Up

(107) 

1. Hold the tone for 20 counts.
2. Expel any air remaining in lungs.
3. Do not breathe for 20 counts.
4. Inhale.
5. Repeat the sequence.
6. Apply to playing the scale.

## Scale

(Harmonic Minor)

(108) 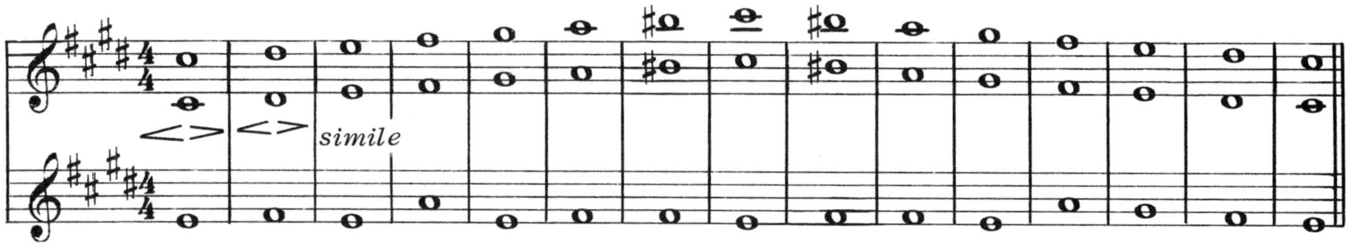


(109) 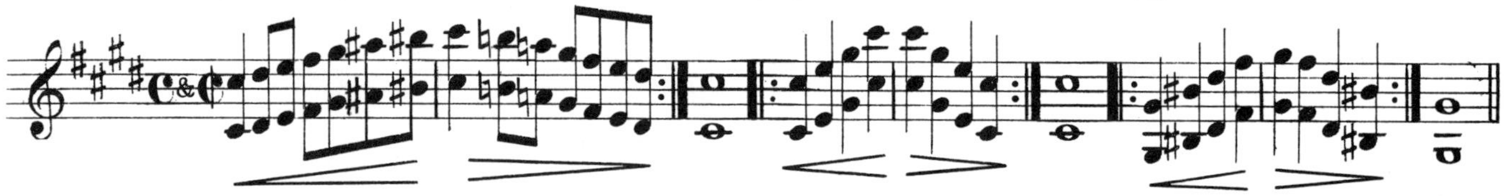


## Chord Study

(110) 

## Intervals

(111) 

## Etude

Rhythms 

Andante ①

Barret (adapted)

(112) 

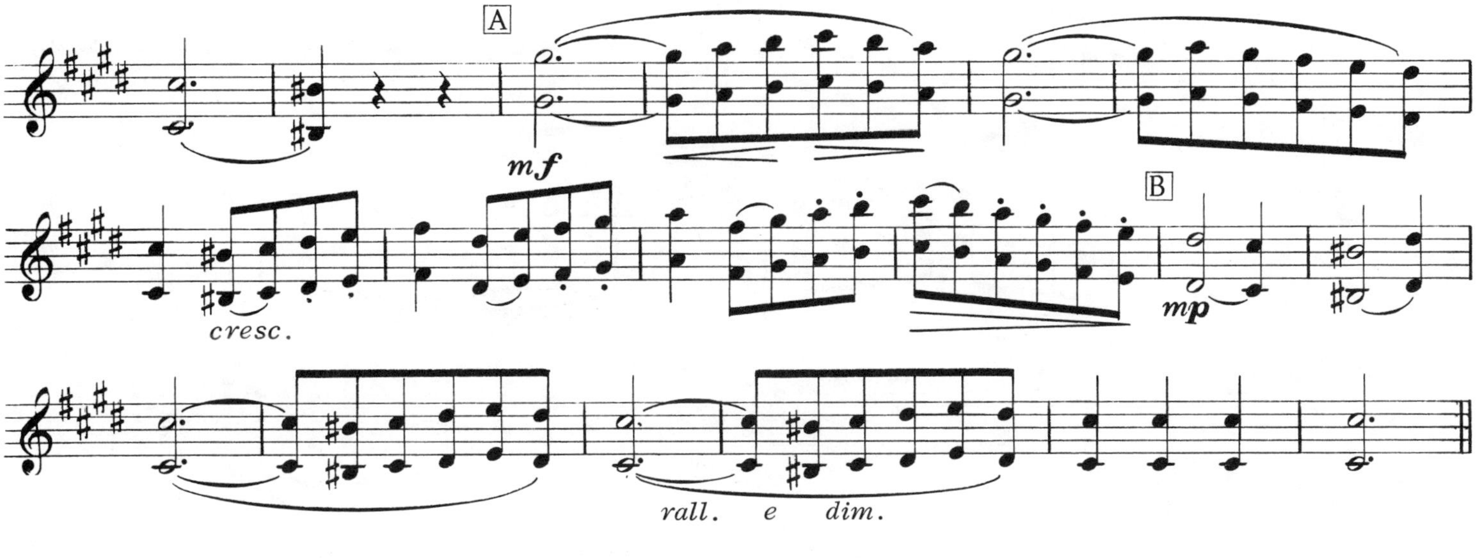


## Accompaniment for Etude

Andante

## E♭ Major

(G♭ Concert)

Breathing and Warm Up

113 

1. Hold the tone for 25 counts.
2. Expel any air remaining in lungs.
3. Do not breathe for 25 counts.
4. Inhale.
5. Repeat the sequence.
6. Apply to playing the scale.

## Scale

114 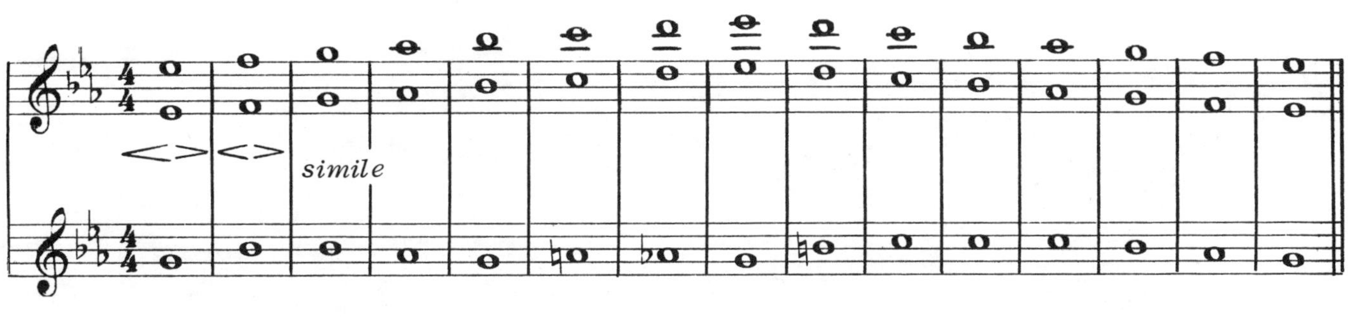

## Study

115

115 Articulations

## C Minor

(E♭ Minor Concert)
(Relative to E♭ Major)

Breathing and Warm Up

116

1. Hold the tone for 25 counts.
2. Expel any air remaining in lungs.
3. Do not breathe for 25 counts.
4. Inhale.
5. Repeat the sequence.
6. Apply to playing the scale.

## Scale

(Harmonic Minor)

117

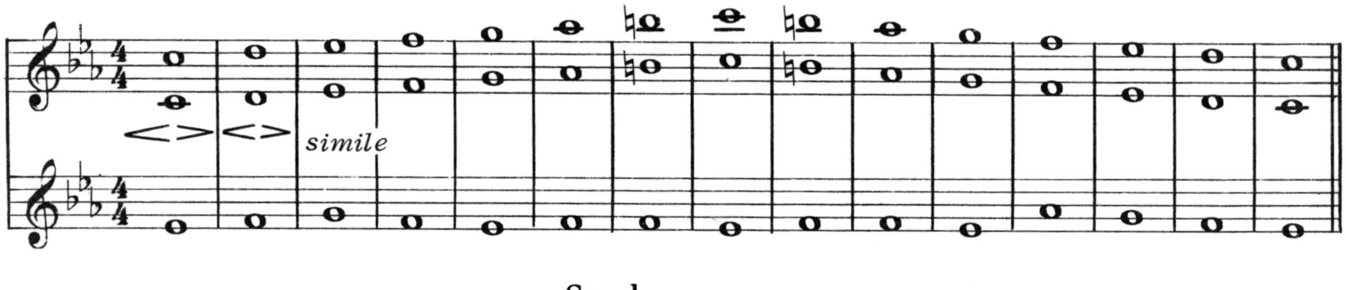


## Study

118

118 Articulations

# B Major
(D Concert)

Breathing and Warm Up

119 

1. Hold the tone for 30 counts.
2. Expel any air remaining in lungs.
3. Do not breathe for 30 counts.
4. Inhale.
5. Repeat the sequence.
6. Apply to playing the scale.

## Scale

120 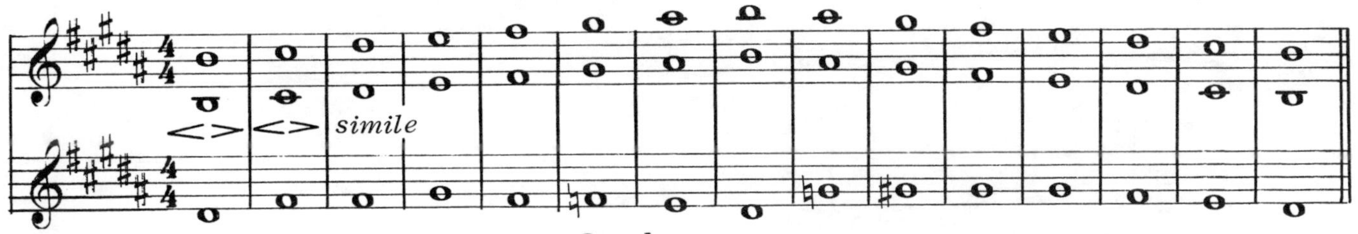


## Study

121 

121 Articulations

# G♯ Minor
(B Minor Concert)
(Relative to B Major)

Breathing and Warm Up

122 

1. Hold the tone for 30 counts.
2. Expel any air remaining in lungs.
3. Do not breathe for 30 counts.
4. Inhale.
5. Repeat the sequence.
6. Apply to playing the scale.

## Scale
(Harmonic Minor)

123 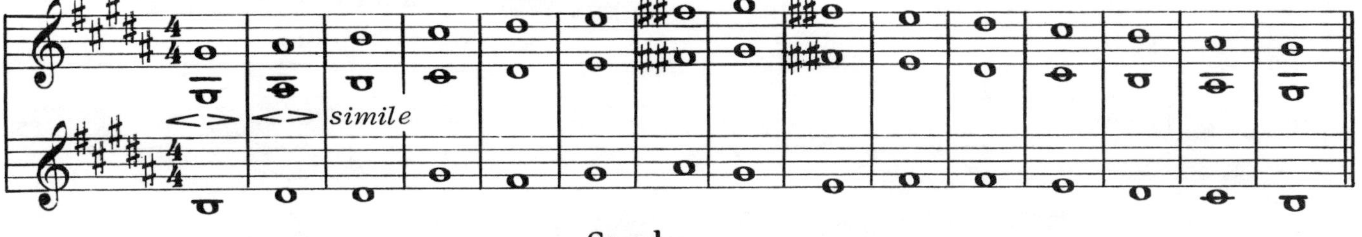


## Study

124 

124 Articulations

# Velocity and Articulation Studies

St. Jacome
(adapted)

125

125 Articulations

Collinet
(adapted)

126

126 Articulations

Pares
(adapted)

127

127 Articulations

Auber
(adapted)

128

128 Articulations

## Syncopation Rhythms

(Play the Harmonized Scales with these rhythms)

129

## Latin Rhythms

(Play the Harmonized Scales with these rhythms)

Rhumba

130

Beguine

131

Tango

132

Samba

133

Conga

134

Mambo

135

Cha Cha

136

Merengue

137

Bolero

138

## Stage Band Rhythms

(Play the Harmonized Scales with these rhythms)

139

## Uncommon Rhythms

(Play the Harmonized Scales with these rhythms)

# Embellishments

The correct use of ornaments in music is a subject in itself. Consequently, only those embellishments most often used can be incorporated in this book. There are exceptions to the rules for performing these embellishments, but they are too numerous to define in the limited space allotted.

The Long Grace Note (Appoggiatura). The length of the Long Grace Note is taken from the principal note. The principal note is not accented.

147

The Short Grace Note. Play as quickly as possible borrowing the little time consumed from the principal note. The principal note retains its proper accent.

148

(Note: In modern usage, it is common for the short grace note to be played in a slight anticipation of the principal note.)

The Double Grace Notes (Double Appoggiatura). Play rapidly, so that no value seems to be taken from the principal note. The principal note retains its proper accent.

149

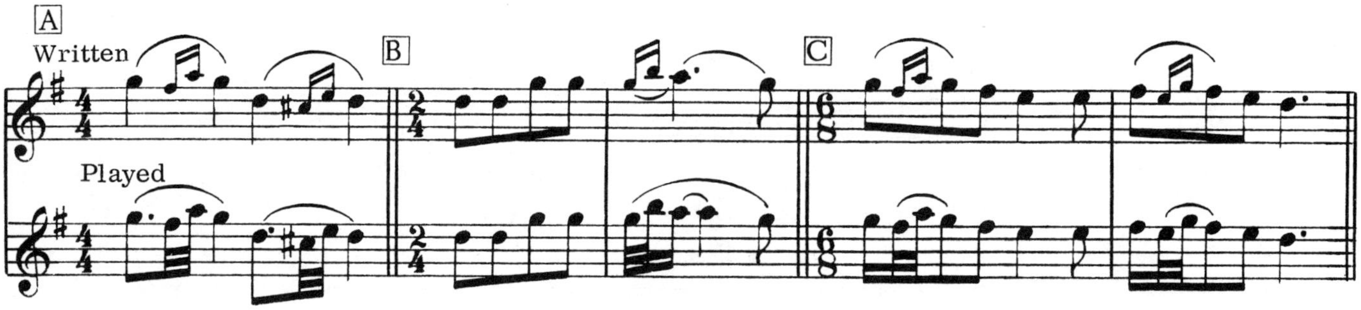


Mordents - Play the first two notes very quickly, holding the third note until the time of the principal note is consumed.

150

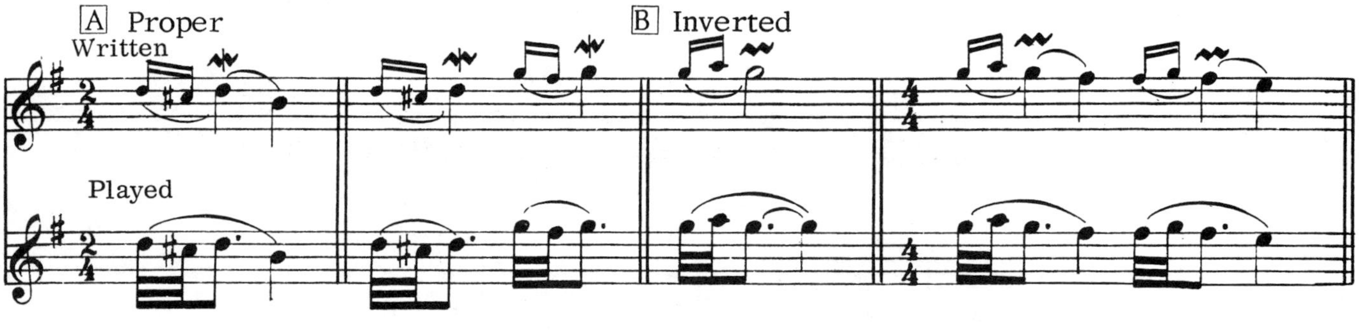

The Turn (Gruppetto). A group of grace notes surrounding any desirable principal note. It should be played broad in slow tempo - light and flowing in fast tempo. All turns should be played legato, and never separated from the principal note.

151

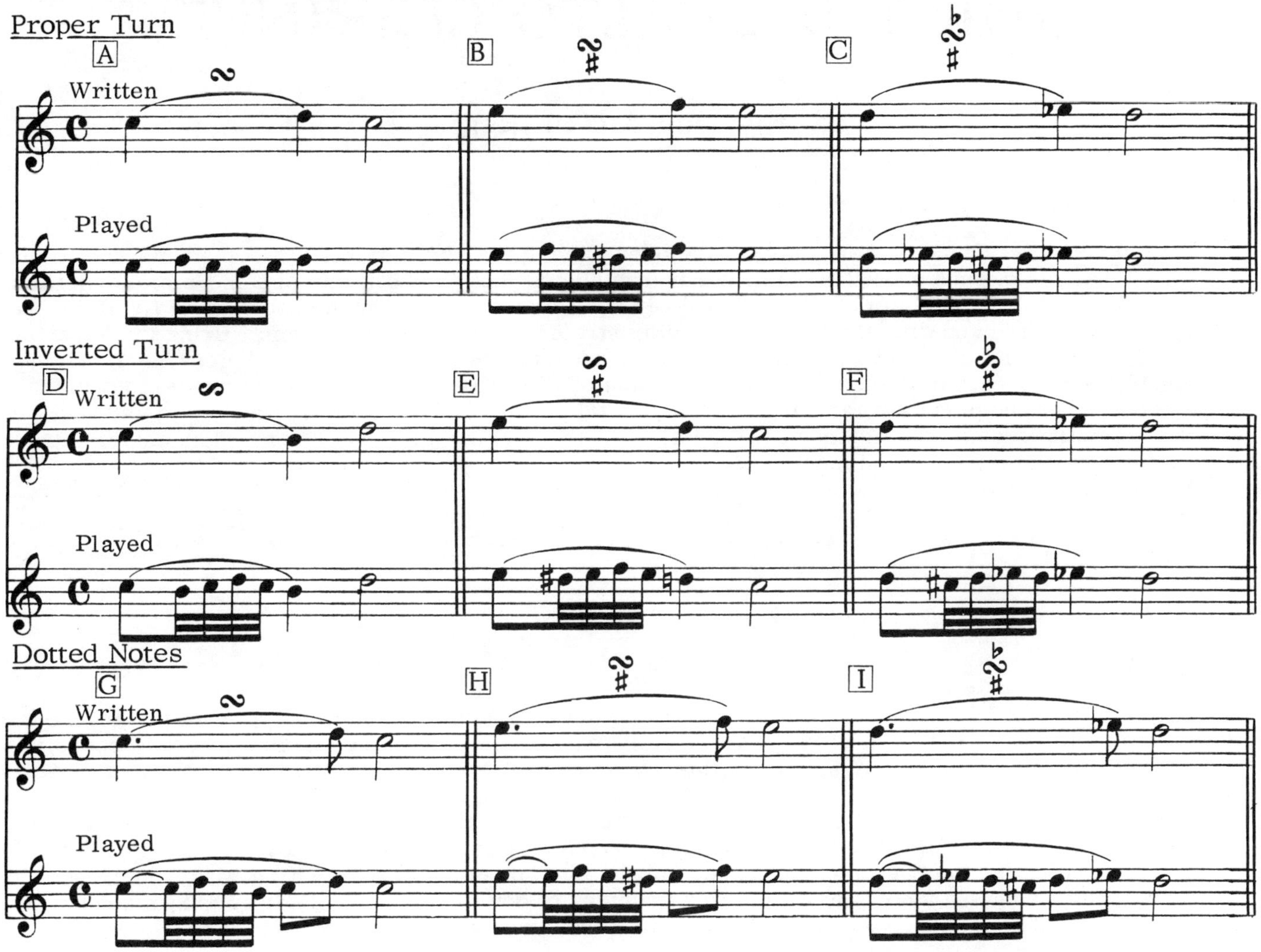


## The Trill

The trill (or shake), indicated by the sign *tr*~~~, is a rapid alternation of a note so marked with the note on the next degree above it.

152

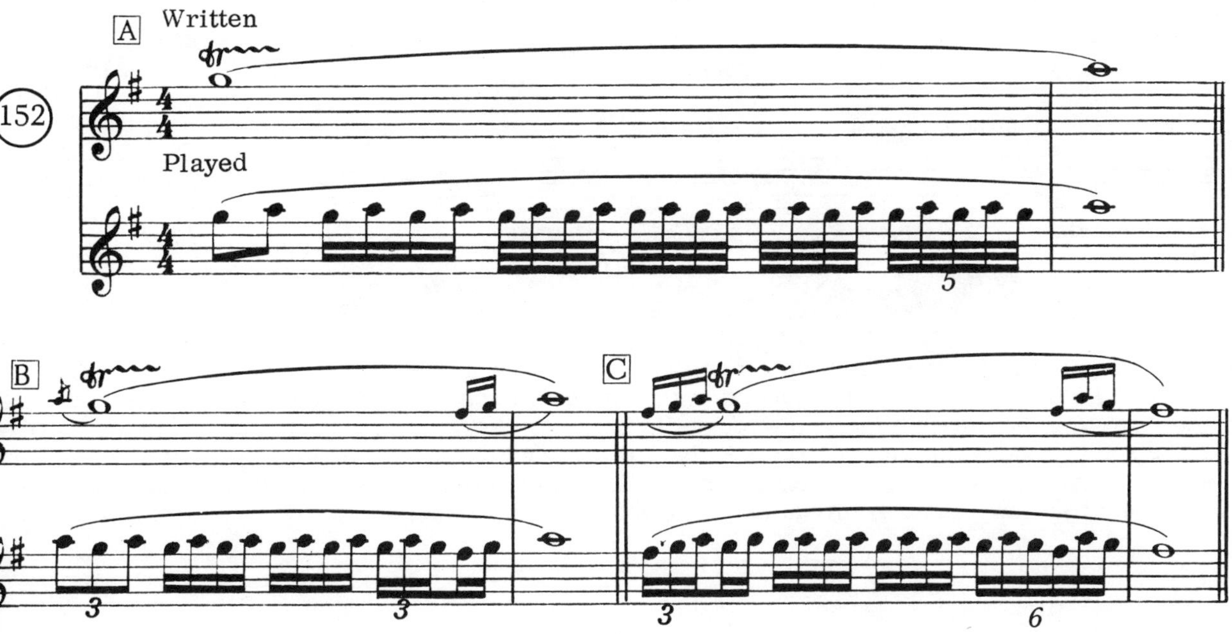

# SPECIAL STUDIES FOR THE E♭ ALTO CLARINET

## by Don McCathren

1. EMBOUCHURE CHECK - Although you have been playing the alto clarinet for some time now, correct embouchure is of such great importance that it is a good idea to check this at this time. Form the embouchure by holding the alto clarinet directly in front of the body, rest the upper teeth firmly on the top of the mouthpiece and drop the jaw with the skin stretched firmly over the chin. Bring the lower lip up to the reed holding the chin down and forward. Close the lips around the mouthpiece as if saying the word "who". To get the proper feel of the amount of pressure or support to use on the mouthpiece, play A♭ concert on the piano and then practice playing this pitch on the mouthpiece alone. Adjust the position of the mouthpiece and the tightness of the lips until the correct pitch can be played and held. Practice the following exercise on the mouthpiece alone.

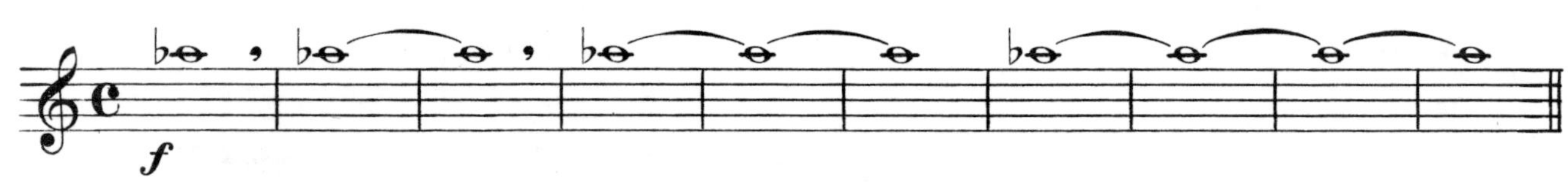


2. LONG TONE EXERCISE - Long tones should be practiced each day to develop a beautiful and well controlled tone. Practice the following exercise making the tone begin and end in silence. Keep the following suggestions in mind when practicing this exercise: 1. Form the embouchure with the lips relaxed. 2. Start the air moving slowly through the clarinet. 3. Gradually tighten the embouchure to make the tone begin. 4. As more and more air is permitted to enter the instrument making the tone louder, the lips must tighten slightly to keep the tone from becoming flat in pitch. 5. Loosen the lips and relax the embouchure as the tone becomes softer so that the pitch does not become sharp. Make the crescendo and decrescendo even and smooth using the same number of counts for each. Begin by using six counts (three up and three down). Add two counts each day until you are holding each tone as long as possible.

3. STARTING THE TONE EXERCISE - To begin the tone beautifully without tonguing noise on the alto clarinet, three steps must be practiced slowly and carefully over and over until they become a habit. These steps are: 1. Placing the tip of the tongue at the tip of the reed. 2. Blowing hard against the tongue (no air goes through the clarinet since the tongue is blocking the opening). 3. Drawing the tongue back to release the air and start the tone. Practice the following exercise performing each step as it is numbered in the exercise. Repeat each measure until the tone can be started perfectly. Stop the tone cleanly and suddenly by drawing the air in quickly at the end of each tone.

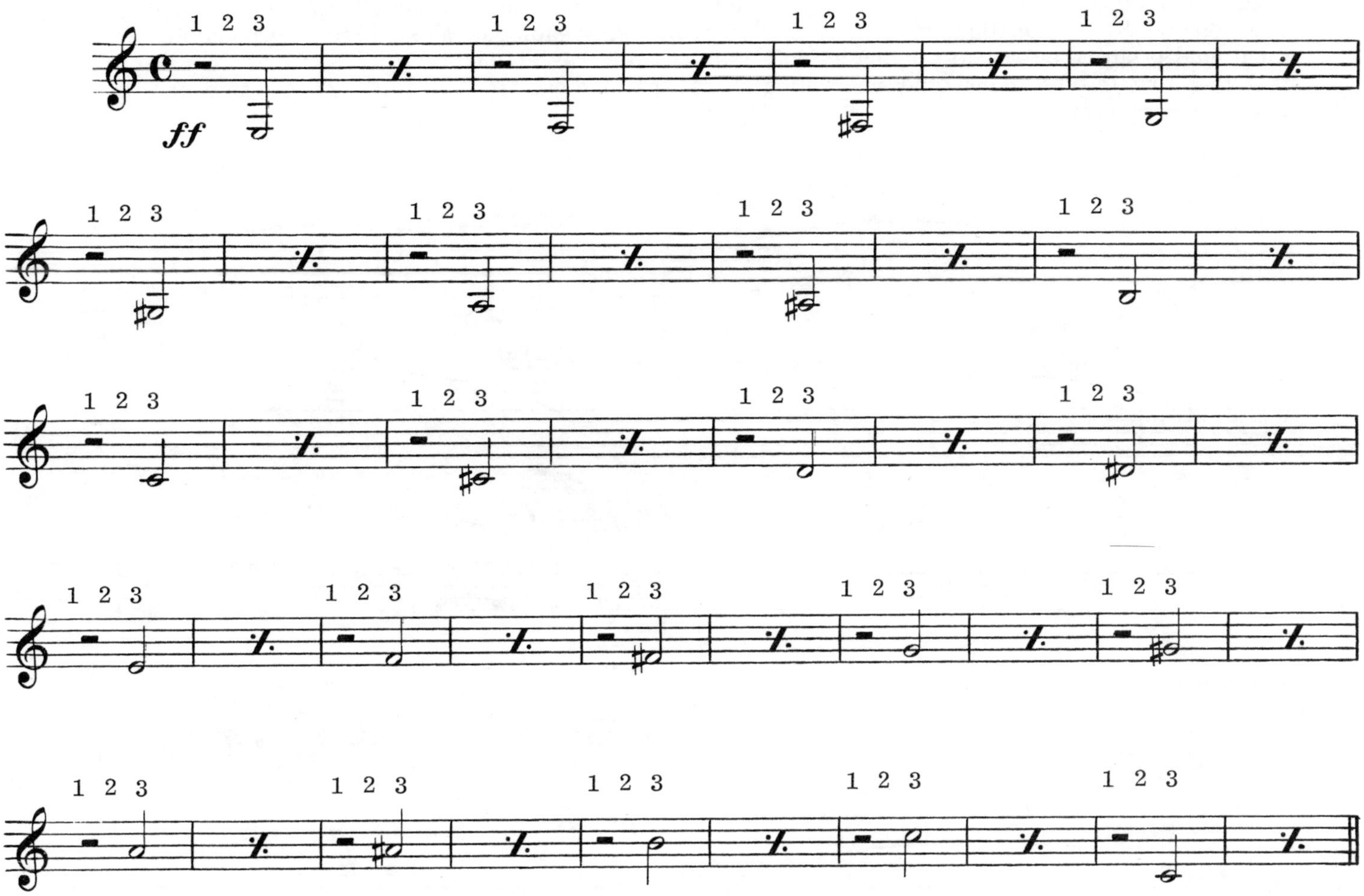


4. LEGATO TONGUING EXERCISE - To develop a fast light tongue, legato tonguing exercises should be practiced. To learn this important style of tonguing, touch the tip of the reed with the tip of the tongue as lightly as possible as if saying the syllable "lah". Do not stop the breath when you tongue legato. Practice the following exercise making the tongue so light that it can just be heard.

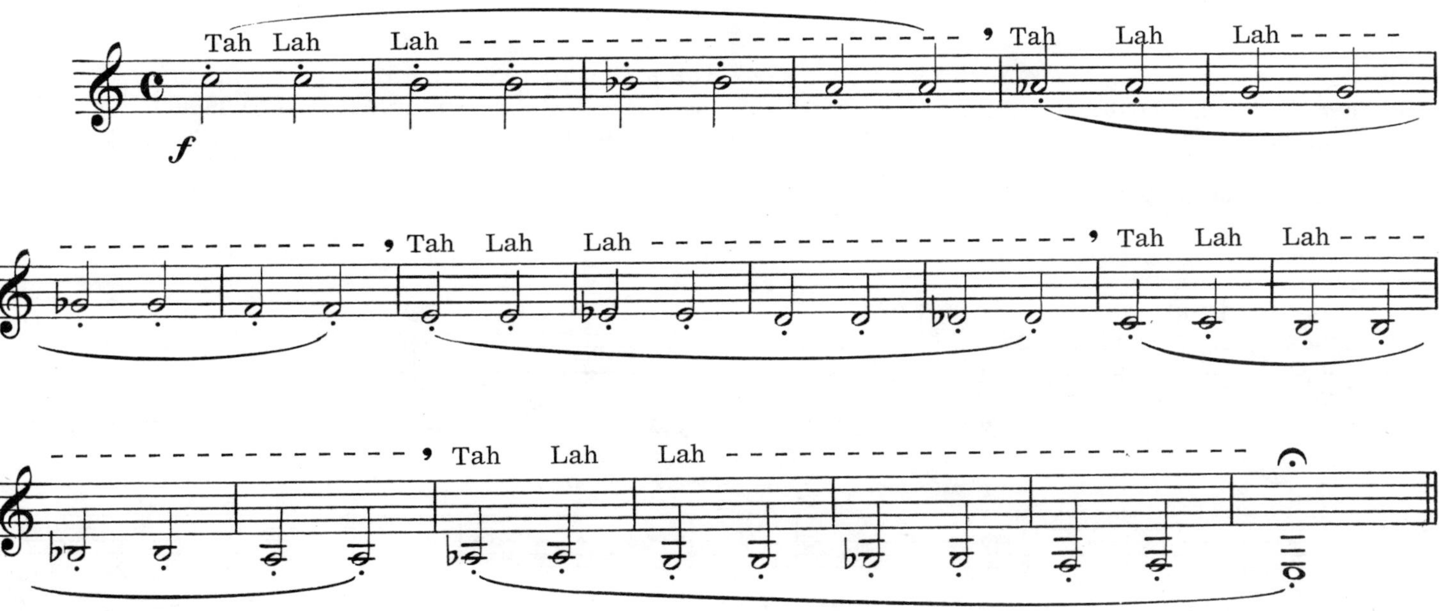

6. TONE QUALITY, INTONATION, FLEXIBILITY AND CONTROL EXERCISES - These elements are of great importance in fine clarinet playing. The following exercises are very helpful in developing excellent tone quality, intonation, flexibility and control. Play each passage as loud as possible with good tonal quality and then repeat playing as soft as possible. Listen carefully to the tones to make certain that they are in tune, connected smoothly and that the tone quality is beautiful. Practice one line each day.

7. STOPPING THE TONE EXERCISES - There are three methods of stopping the tone on the clarinet. All three methods should be mastered to play the clarinet beautifully and artistically. The usual method for stopping the tone is to just stop the air. This causes the tone to decrescendo and die away gradually. This is the same method that was used to stop the tone in the long tone exercise. Practice the following exercises using this method and then stop the notes at the ends of the phrases in your music in the same manner.

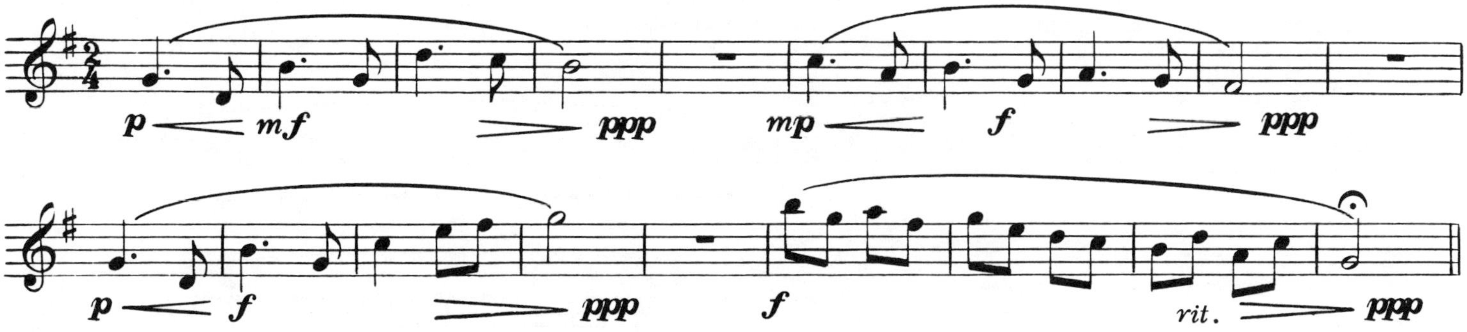


The second method for stopping the tone is by breathing in suddenly. This is used in playing slow staccato passages to stop the tone cleanly and without noise or decrescendo. Practice the following exercise stopping the tone in this manner.

The third method for stopping the tone is with the tongue. This technique is called "stopped staccato" and is used in fast staccato passages. To learn this method of tonguing, start the tone by removing the tongue from the reed and then stop the tone by replacing the tip of the tongue to the tip of the reed while continuing to blow. Practice the following exercises to master this important technique.

7. EXERCISES FOR CROSSING THE "BREAK" - To develop a smooth rapid technique you must spend much time in slow careful practice to learn to roll the first finger to the throat A and G♯ keys without disturbing the basic left hand finger position. Make certain that the first finger of the left hand is curved so that the side of the finger is positioned over both the A and G♯ keys.

8. EXERCISE FOR CHANGING REGISTERS - You must also learn to tip the thumb on to the register key without changing the basic position of the thumb. The following exercises are designed to develop this important technique.

9. EXERCISES COMBINING ROLLING THE FIRST FINGER AND TIPPING THE THUMB -

TO BECOME A FINE PLAYER CHROMATIC FINGERINGS MUST BE LEARNED AND MASTERED. THE FOLLOWING EXERCISES ARE DESIGNED TO ASSIST IN THIS IMPORTANT PHASE OF CLARINET TECHNIQUE.

10. CHROMATIC F♯ EXERCISE - Practice this exercise playing the F♯ first with the thumb and two bottom side keys ([12] and [13]). Next practice the exercise using the first finger of the left hand for the F♯. Practice until you can play smoothly and evenly with either fingering. In chromatic passages you may use whichever fingering seems best for you.

11. CHROMATIC B AND F♯ EXERCISE - In this exercise finger the low B and the high F♯ or G♭ using the chromatic fingering (T-1-2-3-4-[15]). This fingering should be used whenever these notes are found in chromatic passages.

12. CHROMATIC D♯-E♭ AND A♯-B♭ EXERCISE - Finger the low D♯-E♭ and the high A♯-B♭ in this exercise with the chromatic fingering (T-1-2-[14]). This fingering should be used whenever these notes are found in chromatic passages.

13. FORKED FINGERING EXERCISES - Some chordal passages can be greatly simplified if E♭-B♭ and D♯ - A♯ are fingered with the thumb, the first finger of the left hand and either the first or second finger of the right hand. Learn these fingerings and use them in fast technical passages.

14. EXERCISE FOR KEEPING THE RIGHT HAND DOWN - When passing from notes needing the right hand to any of the four throat tones (G, G♯, A and B♭), keep the right hand down for smoother and easier execution. In the following exercise the sign ⊢——⊣ will serve to remind you to keep the right hand down. It is an excellent idea to mark similar passages where the right hand may be kept down in any other music you are playing.

15. EXERCISES FOR THE LOW E♭ KEY - Many alto clarinets have a low E♭ key which is located just below the right hand low E key. This key is used to play low E♭ and may also be used as an optional fingering for the middle or throat B♭. It may be used to excellent advantage in some technical passages. These exercises are designed to help you become familiar with the use of this key. Play all the low E♭'s and throat B♭'s using the low E♭ key.

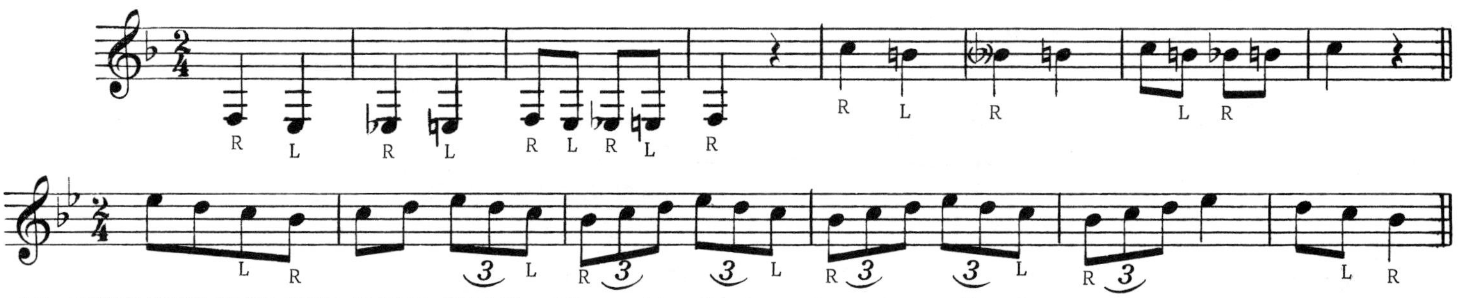

16. EXERCISE FOR THE HALF-HOLE - Many alto clarinets have a small hole in the first finger plate for the left hand. This hole is to be opened by a slight rolling motion of the first left hand finger. The following exercise will help you gain control of this important technique.

17. SLURRING EXERCISES - A fine player is able to slur smoothly blending one note into the one that follows. To develop this important ability, practice the following exercises slowly, moving the fingers slowly and putting them down lightly on the keys and tone holes. Make certain no other notes are heard.

18. VIBRATO EXERCISES - Vibrato is often used in alto clarinet playing and should be learned by all alto clarinet players. Vibrato should be produced on the alto clarinet by dropping the jaw to lower the pitch and raising the jaw to raise the pitch. This action is very similar to chewing and the same muscles are involved. Pronouncing the syllables "Ah" and "Ooo" will give the desired motion. First practice making the vibrato on low C to get the "feel" of producing it. Make the vibrato slow and wide bending the tone as far as it will go without breaking. Next practice the following exercise using one vibrato per beat. After this can be done evenly and smoothly, practice with two vibratos per beat, then three, four and finally five. Approximately one week should be devoted to each step in the development of the vibrato.

Now practice each note of the above scale starting the vibrato very slowly, getting gradually faster until the vibrato is made as fast as possible. Then, gradually slow the vibrato down. Make the vibrato more narrow as it is speeded up and wider as it is slowed down. Each tone should sound like the following diagram:

You are now ready to use the vibrato in the other music you are playing. Practice the following exercise using vibrato on each note that is a quarter note or longer. You should use the number of vibrato pulsations that sounds the most pleasing to you.

19. <u>DAILY EXERCISE ON THE MAJOR TONIC CHORDS IN ALL KEYS</u> - This daily exercise on the tonic chords in all keys should be practiced each day to develop a smooth and rapid technique. Practice the exercise slowly giving one count to each note making certain that the notes are connected smoothly with no additional notes between the notes written. After you have learned the exercise playing the notes in this fashion, practice it as written with two notes to each beat. Later you may play it in cut time with four notes to a beat. For added control, practice the exercise as loud as possible and as soft as possible. This exercise should be practiced slurred in the beginning but later when it can be played in sixteenth notes it makes an excellent tonguing exercise when it is tongued either staccato or legato. Be certain to use all the special fingerings that you learned in the other exercises when playing this exercise. Reminders for the use of these fingerings are included in the exercise. The sign ⊢—⊣ is a reminder to keep all or part of the right hand down across the throat register.

# TRILL CHART

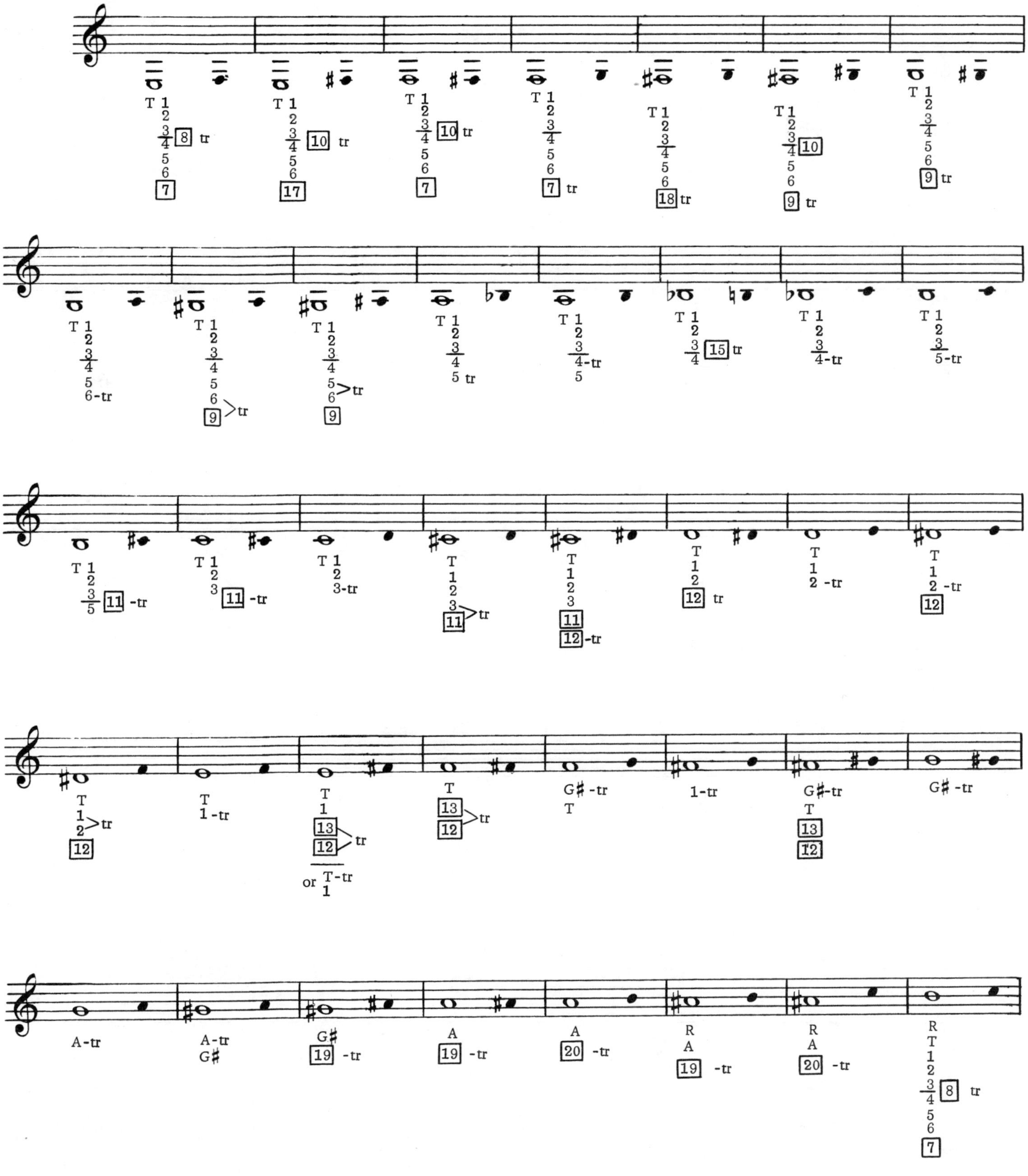
T 1 2 3 4 8 tr 5 6 7
T 1 2 3 4 10 tr 5 6 17
T 1 2 3 4 10 tr 5 6 7
T 1 2 3 4 5 6 7 tr
T 1 2 3 4 5 6 18 tr
T 1 2 3 4 10 5 6 9 tr
T 1 2 3 4 5 6 9 tr
T 1 2 3 4 5 6-tr
T 1 2 3 4 5 6 9 >tr
T 1 2 3 4 5 6 >tr 9
T 1 2 3 4 5 tr
T 1 2 3 4-tr 5
T 1 2 3 4 15 tr
T 1 2 3 4-tr
T 1 2 3 5-tr
T 1 2 3 5 11 -tr
T 1 2 3 11 -tr
T 1 2 3-tr
T 1 2 3 11 >tr
T 1 2 3 11 12-tr
T 1 2 12 tr
T 1 2 -tr
T 1 2 -tr 12
T 1 2 >tr 12
T 1 -tr
T 1 13 12 tr or T-tr 1
T 13 12 >tr
G♯ -tr T
1-tr
G♯-tr T 13 12
G♯ -tr
A-tr
A-tr G♯
G♯ 19 -tr
A 19 -tr
A 20 -tr
R A 19 -tr
R A 20 -tr
R T 1 2 3 4 8 tr 5 6 7

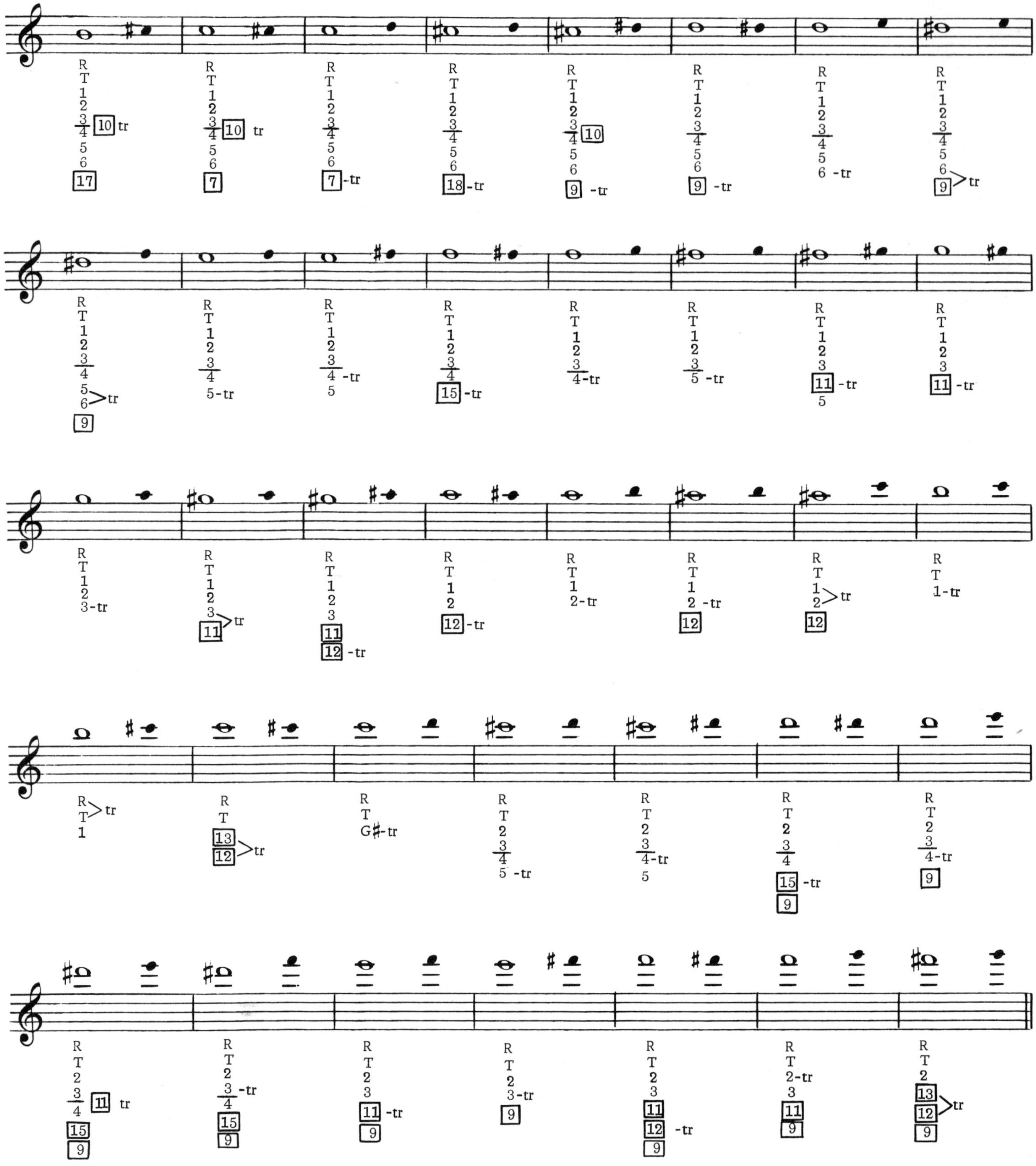
R T 1 2 3 4 [10] tr 5 6 [17]
R T 1 2 3 4 [10] tr 5 6 [7]
R T 1 2 3 4 5 6 [7]-tr
R T 1 2 3 4 5 6 [18]-tr
R T 1 2 3 4 [10] 5 6 [9] -tr
R T 1 2 3 4 5 6 [9] -tr
R T 1 2 3 4 5 6 -tr
R T 1 2 3 4 5 6 > tr [9]
R T 1 2 3 4 5 6 > tr [9]
R T 1 2 3 4 5-tr
R T 1 2 3 4 -tr 5
R T 1 2 3 4 [15] -tr
R T 1 2 3 4-tr
R T 1 2 3 5 -tr
R T 1 2 3 [11] -tr 5
R T 1 2 3 [11] -tr
R T 1 2 3-tr
R T 1 2 3 > tr [11]
R T 1 2 3 [11] [12] -tr
R T 1 2 [12]-tr
R T 1 2-tr
R T 1 2 -tr [12]
R T 1 2 > tr [12]
R T 1-tr
R T > tr 1
R T [13] [12] > tr
R T G#-tr
R T 2 3 4 5 -tr
R T 2 3 4-tr 5
R T 2 3 4 [15] -tr [9]
R T 2 3 4-tr [9]
R T 2 3 4 [11] tr [15] [9]
R T 2 3 -tr 4 [15] [9]
R T 2 3 [11] -tr [9]
R T 2 3-tr [9]
R T 2 3 [11] [12] -tr [9]
R T 2-tr 3 [11] [9]
R T 2 [13] [12] > tr [9]